God Called Collect
from Cleveland

God Called Collect from Cleveland

Remember God y just an outstretched hand away

Denny Mc

Dennis J. McNicholas

ISBN: 0692915346
ISBN 13: 9780692915349
Library of Congress Control Number: 2017910508
Dennis J. McNicholas, Lombard, Illinois

Dedication

This book would not have been possible without the support and encouragement of my most talented and beautiful wife of 43 years, Karin; our three outstanding children, Bridget, Matt and Meghan; and the presence in my life of our five grandchildren: Jack, Gracie, Conan, Liv, and Gryffin, who have made me young again.

Contents

THE ARC OF many lives often seems to feel like a series of journeys, each a going out and a coming back. For some, these circles of life are more concentric, under control, devolving upon each other toward a common goal or center point. For others, these journeys overlap, with no clear beginning or end.

> Midway through the journey of our life, I found
>   myself in a dark wood, for I had strayed
>   from the straight pathway to this tangled ground.
> How hard it is to tell of, overlaid
>   with harsh and savage growth, so wild and raw
>   the thought of it still makes me feel afraid.
> Death scarce could be more bitter. But to draw
>   the lessons of the good that came my way,
>   I will describe the other things I saw.[1]

1 INFERNO: A NEW VERSE TRANSLATION, by Dante Alighieri, translated by Michael Palma. Copyright ©2002 by Michael Palma. Used by Permission of W. W. Norton & Company, Inc. Canto I; page 3.

Prologue

Chicago
January 22, 1974

IT FELT LIKE law school all over again, those dreaded bar review classes running six hours a day, six days a week. It was winter, and by the time I finished the last class of the day and exited the building onto Madison Avenue at its intersection with Michigan Avenue, it was already dark — not to mention cold and wet.

A sleety rain drove at a piercing angle as I prepared to make my way to the old Chicago and North Western Railroad station on the corner of Madison and Canal. Madison and Michigan is a grand corner, at least on sunny days: Lake Michigan beckons across Grant Park to the east, and to the south the massive bronze lions standing guard over the Art Institute of Chicago. Looking west, Madison Avenue is like the base of the cavern caused by the flow of the Colorado River, with walls of brick, metal and glass instead of jagged rock. In the morning rush hour masses of people pour from the station and flow east. In late afternoon, the process reverses and the avenue is like a tidal pool, collecting all the currents and channeling them into a swift, mighty river of commuters heading west.

It was around 4:30 p.m. when I entered the torrent. But for the traffic signals there was no stopping allowed. I joined the throngs along the north side of the street that led to the entrance of the station just west of the Chicago River. As I passed the monolith of St. Peter's Church, I thought I heard someone calling my name.

"Dennis! Dennis!"

I stopped and turned toward the church, causing the pedestrians around me to grumble and shove as they tried to move past me. Staffed by Franciscan friars whose living quarters are above the main level, St. Peter's offers a unique place of quiet and sanctuary in the midst of the bustling city. The main entrance has a series of steps leading to a large set of beckoning bronze doors. I could see a few dark figures huddled on the steps — homeless people in ragtag blankets — but no one that I recognized. The grey, fading light of afternoon didn't help.

"Dennis!" This time, a man emerged from the shadows of the steps and came toward me. "Dennis, it's Pat. Pat Murphy."

"Pat? Is that you?"

I hardly recognized him. The last time I saw him was three years earlier when we were finishing our military police training at Fort Gordon. This Pat was considerably heavier, his unkempt hair grayed and in strands that clung to the neck of a damp, tattered shirt. He was caked in filth; partly his own, partly the dirt of the city, all of it mixed into a wicked brew. The squishy sound of rainwater leaked from his socks and out through shoes held together by wire. Long, blackened nails protruded from the remnants of fingerless gloves. His teeth, when he smiled, were coated with a greenish-yellow substance. What unbalanced me the most were his eyes — they revealed nothing, neither shame nor joy. They sat empty in their sockets.

"What are you doing here?" he asked, as if it were only natural to find him this way, but not me.

"I have a class near here," I told him, still not comprehending what could have happened to this once-robust, charming man. "What about you?" I asked politely.

"I'm staying at a shelter run by Father Marquardt. It's two blocks south, but I like to say a few prayers here every day."

I didn't know quite how to phrase all the questions I had. "How did you get here?" I asked.

"I was out in Washington State and my sister came to get me. We got as far as Chicago and I decided to stay here."

"But you can't stay *here*," I said, looking around at the huddled figures on the church steps. "Come with me. I'm sure we can find you somewhere better." I put my arm around his shoulder and he offered no resistance, but he said he hadn't said his prayers yet. He couldn't leave without saying his prayers.

"Let's get you cleaned up first," I said. "Then you can pray."

We certainly made an odd couple as I took him to board the West Line train— me in my suit and tie, and Pat sending people scurrying away from him. Although the cars were packed with homeward-bound commuters, Pat and I soon had the upper level mostly to ourselves as the other passengers retreated from the sight and stench of Pat. I, too, had difficulty engaging in normal conversation while trying to ignore the smell that magnified and radiated in the heated car.

I didn't know exactly what I would do with Pat, but I couldn't let him go back to that shelter. It was only open at night, and only served dinner and then breakfast in the morning. After 7 a.m., Pat was on his own all day, without food or shelter. Chicago offered few public restrooms for someone like him. I wondered when his last shower had been.

We carried on a semblance of a conversation. Pat spoke in high decibels, as if he had just come off the firing range at Fort Gordon without having used his standard-issue earplugs. His foot coverings dripped melting black slush over the railing where he put his feet up, and down onto the unfortunate passengers in the lower car. I tried to reposition him without calling attention to why I was doing it.

After 40 minutes, we exited the train at the Lombard station where I was living for now with my parents. I did not yet own a car, and apologized to him for the two-mile walk still ahead of us. "It's slightly longer than the run we took every night at Fort Gordon," I said.

"Haven't been running much lately," he said. It was the closest he came to acknowledging his changed situation.

During the walk, I began to worry about what I had done by rashly inviting Pat home. It was one thing for me to offer help, but another to expect the same from my parents. "I hope you don't mind, but I'm going to have to ask you to take your shoes off before we go inside," I told Pat.

When I opened the front door with my key, I stood in the way so as to block my parents' initial view of my old friend. "Hey, Den," my father called from the living room, where he was watching TV.

"I want you both to meet someone," I said. "This is Pat Murphy, my bunkmate from the Army. What are the chances I'd bump into him on my way to the train?"

My mother came into the living room when she heard my voice. She had begun to greet me, but stopped in mid-sentence. My father just stared from the living room.

"Say hello," I prodded them.

"I'm sorry, hello," said my dad.

My mother drew herself up, and I loved her at that moment more than any other time in my life. "Welcome to our home, Pat," she said.

I asked Pat if he'd like to clean up, and to my great relief, he said yes. My father went to fetch a robe for him, and after Pat handed his clothing through the bathroom door to me, my mother put his shirt and pants directly into the washing machine. The socks and underwear went right into the garbage.

My sister, Maureen, 19, wasn't home. My youngest brother, Kieran, 17, was due home any minute, and Kevin, age 24, was on campus at the seminary where he was a student. I found my parents talking in hushed tones in the kitchen.

"I don't blame you for being confused and even upset," I told them. "I don't know what happened to Pat, but I couldn't just leave him out in the cold. I'd like to buy him a ticket tomorrow and put him on a bus to Cleveland, where he has family. Otherwise, I'm afraid he'll die on the streets of Chicago."

"Just make sure he has enough towels," said my mother.

Pat inhaled his dinner as if he hadn't eaten in weeks. He was cleaner than before, but the hot water couldn't wash away the street person he had become. Even when he smiled I could glimpse some of the inner demons that had driven him to this condition. This was not the Pat I had known when we parted at Fort Gordon.

That night, I took him shopping for a shirt and a pair of shoes. He slept in my bed after we returned. I offered to bunk with Kieran, but he wasn't thrilled. "Pat's had some bad luck," I explained.

"Nothing like the bad luck *you're* going to have," Kieran said, "because I'm going to kill you!"

I slept on the couch instead.

The next morning I took him to the Greyhound bus station at the corner of Randolph and Clark in the heart of the city. The floors and benches were worn by the decades and by the millions of travelers who had passed through. Pat wasn't talking much, but he waited obediently while I bought him a ticket and put him on a bus to Cleveland.

"How are you feeling?" I asked him.

"I don't know," he said.

"That's all right. You know you can't stay here out on the streets. Your family will be happy to see you. It's where you grew up, where you have your roots."

He stared straight ahead and said nothing.

I waited to make sure he got on the bus. I saw him find a seat. At the last minute he turned to me through the window and gave me a small wave with two fingers.

His bus moved down the center lane toward lower Wacker Drive. The taillights shone brightly as the bus made its last right turn and disappeared. I wondered if that was the last time I'd ever see my old friend.

CHAPTER 1

·

What a Good Boy Does

I WAS FIVE years old. I wandered down the short hallway from my room to the bathroom, where my father was shaving. "Where are they?" I asked. "Where's Mommy and the new baby?"

My father studied his face in the mirror, perhaps so he wouldn't have to look at me. "Mommy will be back from the hospital soon," he said. "The baby won't be coming with her."

When my brother, Brian, was born, he immediately developed pneumonia and died four days later. My parents must have cried, but I never saw it.

My parents were good people. Maybe I could make Mommy happy if I was a good boy. I always tried to be a good boy and do what good boys were supposed to do.

It didn't always work.

·

The world into which I was born on June 17, 1947, was struggling to recover from World War II. Europe was reeling like a beaten prizefighter. For the first time in more than ten years there was a reduction in open conflict in a world that still seemed clinically dysfunctional.

At least our men and women were home. They'd done their duty, fought the good fight.

I come from a family of servicemen. My father was a war veteran, as were three of my uncles. They suffered no obvious wounds, not the type you can bandage. Their wounds ran deeper.

In the early 1900s, my father's father, John, fled the persecution of the rocky fields of the western coast of Ireland. Having survived the voyage to America, he was faced with the grim reality of World War I: Fight and earn citizenship. He fought. Mustard gas and trauma gave him a perpetual bounce in his leg. Even when he was seated it was obvious, as if he were keeping time to an Irish jig.

John died in a scaffolding collapse in 1926 when my father was six, the oldest of three. My grandma, a poorly educated Irish lass, at once lost her sweetheart, her home, and so much of what had made life here so much better than the grim future she had faced in the Old Country. She and her children became nomads, living with family members until she finally remarried. My father suffered scars from that time, too; only when I became an adult did I begin to understand how many.

By coming from a family of servicemen, I assumed early on that every man must be prepared to fight. The American flag was proudly displayed at so many churches of so many denominations. This was no less common than national flags in the churches of Germany, Poland, Italy, Spain, and France and all nations of the world ravaged by war. In places of worship throughout the world, the flag flies when war is at hand and the people call upon their god to bring about victory, but in each victory there is the victor and the vanquished. In my young world we were the victors. The vanquished were foreign to me — cold and anonymous. Each night at midnight, those few television stations that existed, still in their infancy, ended the day's programming with the American flag unfurled in the wind. No bloodstains or gaping holes from the shrapnel of war marred its beauty as the national anthem played. Some stations even offered a flyover of American warplanes.

This cross-pollination of the DNA of the American flag with religion, perhaps even with the Christian God, seemed so natural to me in the springtime of my life. Only later would I learn that this subtle cross-pollination is a time-worn strategy of governments and ruling classes in their quest for legitimacy. I didn't understand then that God couldn't both win *and* lose a war at the same time, and that men often used God as a symbol and a shield. In my world, there was only the God of victory.

Not long after I was born my parents moved into an apartment building in the Austin District on the west side of Chicago. My Uncle Tom and his wife lived in the apartment upstairs. Our building shared a party wall with the adjoining one, but it didn't seem strange that there were no windows on that side; it was just how people lived. A narrow alley separated our block from the one to the east, like the walls of the heart's chambers.

Everything we needed was within a small radius. It was a three-block walk to church and school. There was a funeral home at the corner on Madison Avenue, a commercial district. The proximity of the buildings, and having to keep windows open for lack of air conditioning, all led to knowing our neighbors perhaps too well, but our world was our block, our neighborhood, our church. Perhaps my parents were more protective because of the chaos they had known, or perhaps it was the church of their ancestors that guided their choices, but the rules of neighborhood, family, and church were like a warm blanket that kept me safe. I thrived in this environment, having known no other.

The brick building's interior contained plaster and wood, lots of wood. The apartment had a musty smell and there were no dehumidifiers. Mold was a wall decoration. There was an unheated enclosed porch with a small room that was large enough for a single bed. If I was really good I was allowed to sleep there on summer nights. I could press my face against the screen to the only window and breathe in the cooler air of night. I had a small wheel and I played a game: I steered the moon so clouds would never fully conceal it.

June 19, 1950: North Korea, aided by the USSR and China, invades South Korea. The United States responds in support of South Korea and suffers 33,741 dead and 103,284 wounded. When we hear "wounded" we often think it's not so bad, at least they're alive. In reality, the wounds suffered in battle are often so catastrophic that the life the wounded knew or dreamt of is stolen from them forever.

I awoke at 6 a.m. on Saturdays to watch *The Big Picture*, which aired from 1951 to 1964 and featured actual combat footage from World War II and the Korean War. With its unseen narrator, this was war in the abstract: glorious, victorious, and impersonal. These were wars I could get behind.

I was six years old and ready to serve. My little rubber cowboys punched each other. My toy rubber soldiers had small guns, hand grenades, and bayonets. Some would "die" until I deployed them again. I supplied the sound effects from the strange yet strangely powerful vocabulary of my favorite Sergeant Rock comic books: BAM. POW. ZING.

Like most little boys back then, I had a cowboy hat and a six-gun with a holster. With Westerns ruling the airways, there was a lot of shooting. I ran around the neighborhood with a toy rifle trying to shoot my friends before they shot me.

Cowboys were heroes. Soldiers were heroes. Killing the bad guy, the other guy, made the world a better and safer place. Killing was clean and impersonal. There was no slow motion and very little moaning or crying out on the part of the victims or the dying. The friends I shot would perhaps clutch their shirts and admit, "Argh, you got me!"

After shooting my friends I would come home and say Mass. My mother would pin one of my small blankets around my shoulders and cut small hosts out of white paper. My brother, Kevin, was only three, and he was usually the only one in our home congregation, seeing as I had already shot everyone else I knew.

All of this took place in my hometown, in my neighborhood. I had no way of seeing the moral storm that was forming on my horizon.

Fourth grade would be my formal entry into the anteroom of clerical life. It was only in fourth grade that one could become an altar boy. First, you had to learn all of the Latin responses to the prayers said by the priest at Mass, so I hurried home from school each day to study with my mother at the tiny white kitchen table. She guided, coached, and encouraged me.

The first boy to learn the Latin responses would be the first to serve Mass, and I became that boy. I had no idea what the words meant in English, but that didn't seem to bother anyone.

Serving assigned Masses was not enough. Benediction took place every Sunday at 4 p.m. I rode my bike to church on occasion to see whether anyone had forgotten to show up so that I could serve.

By the sixth grade, I had something my classmates lacked: utter certainty. I announced to the nuns that I was going into the seminary, following in the steps of my father and uncle.

CHAPTER 2

Young, Like Wet Cement

*1957: Thirteen Americans are wounded in three terrorist bomb-
ings of U.S. installations in Saigon.*

FATHER PHILLIP CAHILL was still on the faculty of Quigley Seminary when I
began my studies there in 1961.

Father Phil, my mother's oldest brother, was the patriarch of our family. One of his first assignments had been to shepherd the young men in
his parish who had also graduated from Quigley, my father among them.

He was a powerful figure both physically and spiritually. He lived a
Spartan-like celibate life. He was loving, firm in his convictions, and happy
in his work. He was intelligent and well respected. He had so much of
what I and many other young men, particularly those in our family, could
only dream of having and being when we became men. He influenced
my family in such profound ways that there was an unspoken expectation
that all the young men in the family would enter the seminary.

Father Phil played basketball with my father, or ping-pong when their
game of choice was not available. My father's mother, Mary, had remarried and now had a home and financial security, but her new husband,
unfortunately, was a drinker who never took a liking to my dad. He dis-
missed young John as someone who would never amount to much. Father
Phil, knowing this, came to the rescue and began to invite young John to
Sunday dinners at his family's home on the South Side of Chicago.

As my father tells it, the first time he saw my mother she was hanging upside down from a tree limb in her backyard. He left the seminary, having completed two of the seven years of study that preceded ordination, and joined the Army Air Corps. He and Ann Cahill were married on January 19, 1946.

My father was pious, loving, caring, and extremely intelligent, but lacked the self-confidence to really better himself — not until he was in his fifties, when he retired from Sears Roebuck and bought a body shop with his son, Kieran (Mac). He was happier than he'd been in decades. But he certainly felt the pull of the priesthood when he was young, as did I. Mine was an idyllic world in which church and state seemed to peacefully if not enthusiastically co-exist. Satan was often depicted as a menacing male with horns, dark features, long fingernails, and an evil but inviting smile, and I was planning to avoid this crime scene at all cost.

I was not alone. While in seminary I was joined by my brother Kevin, as well as five of our cousins. My youngest brother, Kieran, spent a brief time in another seminary.

The building that housed Quigley Seminary was dedicated in 1918. Named after Archbishop James Edward Quigley, this all-male seminary was located at the corner of Rush and Chestnut Streets in Chicago. Its motto, *Ora et Labora* (pray and work), was instilled in each student from the first day of classes.

The most distinctive architectural feature of the school was the Chapel of St. James with its beautiful stained-glass windows, modeled on the Sainte-Chappelle in Paris. In 1996 the building was placed on the National Register of Historic Buildings. I was so proud to be a seminarian, and my parents were so proud of me. I became a member of the choir. At the start of my junior year I was selected as one of eight who were destined to be one of the Cardinal's Servers. These were all things a "good boy" did, although I still wonder even now whether my parents' dream for me was partly that I might finish what my father hadn't, back when he had been the heir apparent to Father Phil.

Rush Street at that time was notorious for its pole dancers, and Quigley had strict rules for its seminarians. Maps were posted at the exit doors advising us which side of the street to walk so as to keep us as far as possible from temptation. We had classes on Saturday instead of Thursday. All of this had a dampening effect on our chances of running into the opposite sex.

As a consequence, all of my friends were male, and I felt awkward to the extreme in the presence of any female who happened to wander into my orbit. My grammar school pal Tom had a sister, Mary Jane, who was a stewardess, which in the early 1960s was as sexy and exotic as you get. Although I was a good student, diligently pursuing my three hours of homework each night, I occasionally went off with Tom when he used the family car to pick up his sister at O'Hare Airport. True, I struggled for entire seconds as I grappled with the moral dilemma of choosing between translating Caesar's Gallic Wars from the Latin, or riding in a car to gaze bashfully at Tom's stewardess sister, but I could not abandon my friend in his moment of need. (When I found out years later that Tom's sister continued into her old age to refer to me as "that kid," I was devastated.)

1963: President Kennedy announces that the United States will increase its aid to Vietnam. By 1963 there are more than 16,000 U.S. advisors in Vietnam. After Kennedy's assassination, President Johnson rapidly escalates the U.S. troop commitment to a total of nearly half a million. This, despite running against Barry Goldwater on the platform that he would not commit more troops to Vietnam.

We were all so young, like wet cement. Father Phil and the other priests on the faculty and at our churches made impressions that for many of us would last a lifetime. We were eager to be men of peace, God's representatives who would cause harm to none. But in the early 1960s the country was changing, and so were we. Puberty arrived. It muscled its way into my life and spiritual path. Although I continued on through my junior and senior years, and spent much time in prayer and in consultation with my spiritual advisors, I wasn't certain by the age of 18 that I would be able to master celibacy the way my uncle had. I wasn't sure I wanted to try.

I wasn't alone in having these qualms. We began our freshman year with 280 members in the class; only 125 graduated. Most of the others left for reasons similar to mine. Those of us who shared these doubts were encouraged to leave the seminary and take time to consider our options. I was sad and deeply disappointed in myself. I was leaving my good friends as we graduated in June 1965. Even though I felt that I might some day return to complete my seminary studies, I felt like I had failed my parents, my family, and Father Phil. It wasn't what a "good boy" was supposed to do.

March 1965: Though not widely publicized and seemingly of little concern to most Americans, 3500 Marines land in South Vietnam. The French have been there before us with disastrous consequences.

I spent one year at Loyola University in Chicago. However, living under my parents' roof no longer provided the satisfaction it had in the days of cowboys and Indians. Several of my friends had enrolled at St. Mary's College in Winona, Minnesota, and in January 1966 I went to visit that campus during the school's winter break.

Chicago was cold in the winter, but it had nothing on Winona. I took the Milwaukee Road train from Union Station, and when I emerged from the eight-hour ride, the setting sun was casting shadows over the valley and the crusted snow gave way with a groan at each step. My lungs constricted as I drew my first breath of bitter-cold air; even the old diesel engine seemed to heave in the crisp air.

Only three of us exited the train at Winona, a small town of 25,000 on the west shore of the Mississippi River, cradled in the womb of the Hiawatha Valley. St. Mary's is slightly west of the city and higher up in the sandstone bluffs that border the campus. I could scratch frost from the window of my taxi as we made the ascent. It was like being inside a snow globe.

I fell in love with the idea of St. Mary's — its setting, the people, the size, and the quiet. I'd been worried that I wouldn't get in. At my initial interview, Brother Frank started off with softball questions, and then changed his tone.

"You know, Dennis, transfer students don't generally do well at St. Mary's," he said. "I think you need to know that before we go any further."

I immediately went back in time to when Sister Padget in the eighth grade called me a fraud in front of my classmates because she thought I had fudged the answer to a question. I hardly heard another thing Brother Frank said, but was relieved when the acceptance arrived a few painful weeks later.

CHAPTER 3

The Drumbeat Gets Closer

1966: There were more than 400,000 American military personnel in and on the waters off South Vietnam. Of them, 6000 have been killed and 30,000 wounded.

A LARGE PERCENTAGE of Americans would have had difficulty locating Vietnam on a map, yet U.S. military advisors had been there since 1950. As our involvement grew it became obvious that there was no place to hide, not even in Winona.

The sister of my roommate, Jack, was dating Mike Tower, a fellow seminarian. He graduated in June 1966, and in October Jack got a letter from his sister saying that Mike had died in a firefight when he threw himself on top of a grenade to protect other members of his platoon.

Mike Tower was the first person I knew to die in Vietnam. I wondered how he could have transitioned from training for the clergy to becoming a Marine, a warrior, so quickly. The question haunted me.

ℳ

St. Mary's proved to be a perfect transition from my years in the seminary. There were numerous Christian Brothers on the faculty and staff, and three seminaries on campus — St. Joseph's, Sacred Heart and Immaculate Heart of Mary. It was an all-male bastion except for some nuns and other women on the faculty or working in the cafeteria. The only girls my age were two miles down the road at St. Theresa's, but they might as well have been 2000 miles away for someone like me with no car, not to mention the very few social skills I had when it came to the opposite sex.

Meanwhile, I was not sure how to contain the growing forces of awareness that began to fight for acknowledgement. By May 1967, the end of my sophomore year at St. Mary's, I had an uncommon sense of freedom, although no real access to girls and no idea what to do should I encounter one. My friends and I, enjoying a magical and uncomplicated existence with no financial, job, relationship, or health worries to speak of, burned off testosterone through playing various sports.

On the other hand, although Vietnam still seemed far away, it was edging into our collective consciousness. A group of us were discussing student draft deferments one hot July night in our usual booth at the Lemon Tree Snack Shop. We hung out there so often hoping to meet girls that the owner had sponsored our softball team.

"Tom, I know you don't have to worry because of your medical condition," said our catcher, John, "The Beast". We all had nicknames. Mine will be disclosed in my will. "What about you, Denny? Do you know what you're going to do when we graduate?"

"I haven't the remotest idea," I said. "I hope I get into some law school and that I'll never have to serve or worry about the war personally."

"Yeah but what do you *think* about the war?" he persisted. "You must have an opinion."

"John, the God's honest truth is that I'm not sure what I think," I said. "Most everyone I know, including most of my family, is in favor of it. I just can't get enthusiastic about any war at all, and I sure don't feel comfortable with the protestors. You're in the seminary, so you don't have to worry about being drafted and having to go into the military."

"I may not ever have to fight but I do have an opinion," he said. "I was contacted by the FBI last week because a friend used my name as a reference for a government job. I wasn't going to say anything, but this FBI guy had a photograph of me taken at an anti-war protest. Can you believe it? So when he said Catholics weren't against the war, and then asked whether I was a good Catholic, I said yes."

As I prepared to return to Winona for my junior year, the war droned on that fall like a perpetual low-grade headache. It was brutally hot at the start of the semester, not exactly what one might think when one thought of Minnesota weather, and the lack of air conditioning made it harder to study and sleep. The air-conditioned library was suddenly a popular place.

Nevertheless, habits are hard to break. I continued to do my best, spending weekend nights studying, always studying, until one Friday evening in October when I heard the proctor of the dorm, Dr. Jamison (who was also one of my professors) put out a call. "Anyone on this floor up for a drink at the Hotel Winona?"

There were only a few of us around, including my roommate, and Tim and Greg across the hall. I joined my voice to the RSVPs.

"Who's that, Denny McNicholas?" Tim said with disbelief. "I thought you didn't drink!"

"I don't," I said, "but wait till I get my shoes on." It was hard to argue that I still needed to study at 10 p.m. on a Friday and also claim to be mentally stable.

We all squeezed into Doc Jamison's car and drove the three miles to the hotel, where each table was lit by a hanging swag lamp the way they do with pool tables. The waitress took our orders, and when she got to me Doc Jamison saved me embarrassment by announcing that I would have a Manhattan.

"That's great," I said, awkwardly. "A Manhattan." Not that I knew what was in such a drink.

When the drinks came, I took a sip. It was awful, but I didn't want to let on, so I continued sipping it slowly, trying not to screw up my face in distaste.

We talked and laughed. About 20 minutes later Doc Jamison put up his index finger and made a swirling motion, like a cowboy signaling for the wagons to circle up. I didn't realize what the signal meant until the waitress brought us all another round.

"Boy, these are good," I heard myself say as I started on my second Manhattan. The room seemed to be getting darker.

"I think I'll stretch my legs," I said, and set off toward the men's room. I didn't want the others to think I couldn't handle my liquor — which I couldn't — so I stopped first at the jukebox on the opposite wall and pretended to pore over the record selection. Then I sauntered, or tried to saunter, over to the cigarette machine, but everyone knew I didn't smoke, so I couldn't hang around there too long. I made a pit stop at the vending machine, where I seemed to study every candy bar on display, as if taking inventory. Finally, hoping that no one from my table was watching, I made it to the men's room, where I did jumping jacks and splashed cold water on my fevered face.

I have never had another Manhattan since.

確

I was confident by now that I wanted to go to law school. My confidence waned only while I was taking the four-hour LSAT test, during which my hands began to tremble and I had trouble writing. This was not a good sign. My hands continued to shake even after I left the hall in which the test was being given. Perhaps the Career Survey I had recently taken was correct in its conclusion that I was best suited to farming.

Everyone else from the test that morning reported having undergone a minor nervous breakdown. It was only later that we learned there had been a 5.4 magnitude earthquake centered in the St. Louis area that morning. It had been the largest earthquake ever recorded in the State of Illinois, and its effects were felt as far away as central Minnesota.

For now I wasn't going to be a farmer.

CHAPTER 4

✑

The Resident Advisor's Dilemma

I STILL WAS able to artfully dodge the issue of the war even as debates about it raged on and off campus. Then the war exploded on January 31, 1968, with the beginning of the Tet Offensive that brought the war to the streets of Saigon as never before.

There were no 24-hour news channels back then. It wasn't until September 2, 1963 that CBS began a nightly 15-minute news program hosted by Walter Cronkite, the most trustworthy and dependable newscaster of his day. On February 27, 1968, he closed his CBS broadcast with words both honest and prophetic: "Who won and who lost in the great Tet Offensive against the cities I'm not sure. The Vietcong did not win by a knockout, but neither did we. The referees of history may make it a draw."

As if there wasn't enough turmoil, on April 4, 1968, Martin Luther King Jr. was assassinated as he stood on the balcony of his motel room in Memphis. A number of St. Mary's students marched in silence through portions of downtown Winona. I led, carrying a cross that was draped in black.

"You marched to honor him?" asked my father sharply when I went home for Easter break. We sat at the kitchen table, now situated in the rear where they had expanded the house. I looked out on the tiny green space of what remained of the yard where we used to practice our golf swing by hitting whiffle balls against the garage.

"Martin Luther King advocated non-violent change," I said, defending myself. "Isn't that a good thing? Better than war?"

"There are those in the news business that say he was a communist."

"Dad, please. Hasn't there been enough violence surrounding the civil rights movement? He advocated peaceful change."

"I think you're wrong."

My family was extremely patriotic and religiously conservative. This was the first real fissure in my otherwise seamless support of their political line.

March 22, 1968: North Vietnamese and Viet Cong troops attack Khe Sanh, South Vietnam. The siege lasts for 77 days before the beleaguered U.S. troops are rescued in what is known as Operation Pegasus. American forces retake Route 9 and end what has been the largest battle of the war thus far.

1968: On June 6, Robert F. Kennedy is assassinated. In August the Democratic Party holds its presidential convention in Chicago. The National Mobilization Committee to End The War in Vietnam, the Youth International Party (Yippies), and the Students for a Democratic Society (SDS) meet in Chicago while the convention is in session. The anti-war movement is picking up momentum.

The cost of my schooling was a constant challenge. In the spring of 1968 I applied for a Resident Advisor position to help alleviate the pressure on my parents. In early May, as I approached the end of my third year, my application was accepted.

As my senior year began in August 1968, my roommate, Terry, and I were the RAs for a dorm floor of 40 freshmen. All of the RAs had to arrive on campus one week before classes began for our orientation and to give us time to get to know one another. The freshmen were to arrive two days later. Two days before classes began Terry and I had our first meeting with the freshmen. They were a homogeneous group of nearly all middle-class Caucasians, and were each randomly assigned a room-mate, but stress cracks soon appeared.

The second Friday night of the semester was my time on duty. Students with female visitors had to keep their doors squarely open until 10 p.m., after which the women were banished from the dorm. As I made my rounds at 10, I noticed the light on in Rich's room. His brother, a senior, was a friend of mine, so I thought I would take extra care to make sure he was all right.

"Rich, what's the subject that has you in on a fine Friday night like this?" I asked.

"World history, and there's plenty of it," he responded.

Rich was a student's student. He sat in bed in his pajamas, already into the second chapter of his textbook. There was a rainbow of colored markers on his nightstand. Red was the most critical color, especially when placed over another color. He had colored so many sentences in red that it seemed to me he could have saved much time and ink if he had instead marked the passages of no significance.

Rich's roommate, Greg, was out on a date. "Well, I'll leave you to your work," I said.

It was around midnight when Rich appeared at my door looking anxious. "What's wrong?" I asked. "Are you ill?"

"No, but I just called my parents and asked them to drive from Rochester to pick me up," he said. "I can't stay here. It's not safe."

"What do you mean? What happened?"

"Greg just got back from his date and he has a gun."

"He's got a *what*?" I had a vision of the freshmen on my watch shooting each other on the first weekend of school. What had possessed me to become a Resident Advisor?

We walked quickly to Rich's room. Greg was standing at the dresser combing his hair. Atop the dresser was a .38-caliber handgun with a leather shoulder holster.

"Hey, Greg," I said as calmly as I could, trying not to alarm him. "What's with the gun?"

"I'm from one of the toughest areas of Cleveland," he said. "I never leave home without a gun."

"But you're here in Winona, Minnesota. Did anything happen tonight?"

It turned out that while he and his date and another couple were strolling downtown, four townies drove by, swearing at them. "I gave them the finger and they turned around and came back," Greg said. "All four of them jumped out of the car and rushed us. I had my manhood to defend and also my date, so I pulled out my .38. You should have seen them run!"

"Er, Greg," I said. "We strongly discourage the possession or use of firearms here at St. Mary's. I'm going to have to take that from you. Do you have any other weapons?"

"Just my backup .38. It's in my dresser."

"I'll have to take that one too. You can claim them when you go home on break."

I managed to assure Rich that his life was not in danger, and as soon as Monday broke I met with the dean, Greg, and with Rich and his parents. We agreed that there was no need for Rich to leave the school, but that Greg would have to find a new roommate. As it turned out we needed to be more specific with Greg, because after the Thanksgiving break he returned to campus with a crossbow. We confiscated it after I found him with a small grill in his dorm room, cooking a rabbit he'd shot. Greg was not invited back for his sophomore year.

ȹ

By late 1968 there were more than 500,000 U.S. troops fighting in Vietnam. The freshmen were, for the most part, indifferent when it came to the war. However, anxiety levels were high. Debates in the Student Union among upperclassmen were heating up in direct proportion to the increased possibility of our being drafted into the military. For most of us seniors, graduation would mean losing our deferments.

In the midst of the turmoil, I busied myself with studies and applications for law school. My dream was to attend the University of Notre

Dame's law school. The cost was prohibitive, but I applied to be a Resident Advisor in the undergraduate dormitories, and when I was accepted to the law school and also to be a Resident Advisor, my path was clear. I was going to Notre Dame.

CHAPTER 5

❦

The Number 73

1969: By April, the death toll of American military personnel exceeds the 33,629 who died during the Korean War.

THE GOTHIC ARCHITECTURE of the building that housed the law school at Notre Dame spoke of its history and tradition. It both looked and felt like a law school should, with green vines spread high and wide over its gray stone walls.

I started my studies there in August 1969, when the war had become like white noise on campus thanks to a "15-minute rule" that limited protests to the form of civil discussions. Still, the war managed to make itself felt. For its part on behalf of the Viet Nam War Moratorium on October 15, 1969, Notre Dame and the neighboring women's college St. Mary's held a vigil service at Sacred Heart Basilica, attended by some 225 students who lit candles and walked in silence across the campus.

In some ways, the Vietnam War was this thing happening someplace far away that we watched each night on TV. In other ways, it was taking on a life of its own, and no one was immune from its reach. On December 1, 1969, the U.S. Selective Service System conducted two televised lotteries to determine which men born between 1944 and 1950 would be called to serve and in what order.

The only television available for general viewing in the entire law school was located on the lower level. There was nervous chatter as I sat in the packed room, feeling completely alone. This wasn't like any other lottery or contest I had known. Here the first men selected were not winners. They were the ones who would lose their freedom, and perhaps their lives.

The program began. There were 366 blue plastic capsules inside a glass container. Each capsule contained a birth date, and each was to be drawn by hand. It was estimated that perhaps the first 120 birth dates selected would be called to serve in the military.

Congressmen Alexander Pirnie (R-NY) began the process. "Mr. Pirnie, can you please draw the first number?" the moderator asked.

The first number was 257, or September 14. Men born between September 14, 1944, and September 14, 1950, would be the first to be called up.

"Mr. Pirnie, can you please choose the second number?"

I couldn't hear the words well. My ears were stopped up by fear, but I could read the dates and numbers as they were posted.

I clenched my fists. It seemed to be going on forever. Some left the room after their birth dates were selected or because they could no longer tolerate the waiting.

"Mr. Pirnie, would you please select the 73rd capsule?"

"The 73rd number is June 17."

I heard nothing more. I didn't need to. June 17 was my birthday.

After leaving the room I leaned against the wall in the hallway to compose myself. My fate was sealed. I would be drafted. There was no one to call; my family, watching back home, already knew.

I wandered around the campus for hours on that cold and windy December night. Ironically, my initial thoughts were not about dying. My primary concern was whether or not I would be able to kill someone else.

After my last exam was completed, I drove home for the holidays. My fondest short-term desires were for home cooking and sleep. Arriving after dark, I sat in the car viewing the lights from inside the house cast shadows on the snow folded into smooth drifts on the lawn. The chimney puffed small strands of smoke, loosely bound like tattered ropes. The snow failed to sense the warmth from inside.

I walked slowly to the door. The chimes, forgotten in the fall cleanup and hanging from an eave, played familiar music for my tired ears. "I'm home," I announced. My mother quickly came from the kitchen with the two things she was rarely without: her apron and a smile.

"You must be exhausted," she said, wrapping her arms around me. "I've fixed a wonderful dinner for all of us."

My father was in the basement doing laundry. Kieran was upstairs and Kevin and Maureen were on their way.

We quickly got into our Christmas rituals. There was shopping to do and last-minute decorations to put up. The airwaves were filled with traditional songs of peace, love and harmony. It wasn't until the Christmas Eve service, as I sat in the dark of church listening to the choir's hymns, that I began to get in touch again with the lottery, my draft number, and my future. As never before, I was struck by the stark difference between the words of scripture and the reality of what was happening in Vietnam. I tried to artfully dodge the slippery slope of uncertainty between the Christian call to love and my call to arms.

Once I was back in South Bend, alone in my room without the distractions of family and the holiday, I began to really feel the moral dilemma I'd been trying to avoid. The abstract had become real. There would be no more deflecting of the issue. Within months I could be fighting in Southeast Asia, being asked to kill my fellow human beings. The time normally set aside for sleep was now just an opportunity to lie in my bed, endlessly questioning. When I did manage to fall asleep, it was to dreams of falling. I found myself sitting on a narrow pillar of rock rising from a canyon like the twin rocks in Canyon De Chelly in Arizona. I peered over the edge, alone in every respect. My lips moved but I wasn't making a sound. I continued my anxious, incessant prayers. As high as I was, God seemed distant and silent. No one could reach me. I thrust my arms into the air in frustration, waking myself when I struck the headboard, finding myself soaked in perspiration.

I sought out Father Bill Lewers, a faculty member at the law school. I'd heard him speak about his opposition to the war. I hyperventilated while waiting for him, feeling the walls closing in even further, constricting the air I was breathing, until finally he called me into his office.

22

"Have a seat, Dennis," he said. "You don't look very good."

The bookcases and flat surfaces were covered with books and papers. In some cases one book was used as a bookmark in another book.

"Father, I got number 73 in the lottery," I told him. "If I'm drafted I don't think I can go through with it. I don't think I can actually kill anyone."

Father Lewers sat back in his worn chair, the sunlight filtering behind him from the window. "You have options, son, although you may not like many of them," he said. "The most radical involves leaving the country, but you'd never be able to return, and you would have to abandon your dream of becoming a lawyer."

"Er, that does sound radical. Are the other options worse?"

"That's a matter of opinion. You could apply for Conscientious Objector status and hope to do some kind of alternative service. Some who select this option become medics but don't carry a weapon."

"That sounds better to me."

"I caution, though, that it won't be easy. I can connect you with a group that assists with the applications."

"And what if my application is denied?" I asked.

"I guess you could go back to option one."

"Or I can refuse to serve," I said. "Either way, I commit a federal crime. Conviction means I can never become a lawyer. So much for the last year and a half of law school."

"There's always the ROTC," said Father Lewers. "A number of your classmates have already signed up. You can finish law school and probably go into the JAG Corps. You would serve as a military lawyer and probably not see combat. The war may even be over by then. Under the circumstances, not a bad outcome."

"All I know is I can't put myself in a position where I may have to train or encourage others to kill, so ROTC is not an option. If someone dies at my hand no one can tell me it's okay or not to worry about it."

Father Lewers offered to get me copies of the Church's published statements on Conscientious Objectors from the Second Vatican Council. There was also a recent statement from the U.S. Conference of Catholic

Bishops on the topic. Ultimately, though, it was a decision no one else could make for me. I would have to pray on it.

Before things got even more complicated, I knew I needed to talk things over with my parents. My brother Kevin picked me up from the train for a weekend visit. Mom had cooked meatloaf for me, one of my favorites, but her happiness at seeing me was dimmed by a telltale puffiness around her eyes. She had been crying.

After dancing around the subject for a while, I finally plunged in. "Mom, Dad, I think we have to talk about the draft," I said. "I'm really relieved that I haven't been inducted yet, but there are other problems. The thing is, I don't think I can submit to the draft."

"What do you mean?" said my father. "Of course you have to submit to the draft."

"Well, I just don't think I can, and I don't know what I'm going to do. I'm lost." It didn't help that I happened to glance at the picture on the mantel of my father in his Army Air Corps tans, holding his parachute with his foot on the wing of his biplane.

My mother put her head down and the tears started to flow.

"I served during World War II, you know," said my father.

"I know, Dad. Don't you think I know that?"

"And we've always taught all of you children to love God and your country, haven't we?"

"Of course. And I do."

"You know we're fighting the Communists, don't you? And do you know what happens if we don't stop them? And of course you know there are others who have served and are still serving, right?"

"Yes, I..."

"And your uncle, Father Phil. He is the most wonderful priest, and isn't he patriotic as well?"

"Sure, but..."

"And what about...?"

"Dad, please! I remember that you voted for Barry Goldwater and that you are not opposed to the war in Vietnam, but please, let me finish.

I have already spoken to Father Lewers at the law school. He's going to help me with my application for Conscientious Objector status."

My father exploded. "My own son is dodging the draft? I can't believe it," he said. "This all started when you marched for Martin Luther King. I told you, Ann. Didn't I tell you? I told you this wasn't like him. This isn't our Denny."

"That is *not* when this started," I said, but he cut me off.

"What do we tell Father Phil?" he said. "What do we tell our entire family and friends? What are they going to think of us?"

"You're not to blame," I said. "Both of you modeled all the right things for me: faith, loyalty, integrity, patriotism. I've lived my life willingly trying to please you. You taught me that my conscience needed to be strong and well formed so I could make the right decisions even if those around me didn't."

"But what happened?" said my mother, finally speaking up. "What went wrong?"

I dropped my head. I was afraid and ashamed, yet I was in a moral grip that wouldn't release me. The moral values my parents had instilled in me were the same values now pushing me to make a choice that was in direct contradiction to much of what they had taught and modeled for me.

I sat across the table from the two most important people in my world. My words were slow and thoughtful but seemed to be spoken by someone else. "This should have been so easy," I said. "I love God and country and I'm not afraid to die. I just don't think I can kill another human being."

I explained the options, and the consequences.

"And what about becoming a lawyer?" my mother asked.

"I cannot be a lawyer if I've committed a felony."

Their heads drooped. Their shoulders slumped. In a very few minutes their lives had changed. The pride they had felt in their son the budding lawyer had turned to the horror of being the parents of a possible felon.

My father sat mute. My mother got up and left the room. We didn't speak again for the rest of the night.

CHAPTER 6

ꝏ

The Letters

EARLY IN JANUARY 1970 I again went to see Father Lewers. I was ready to go ahead with the application for Conscientious Objector status. Bottom line, I had to be able to live with my choices and with myself. If I wasn't good for myself, I would never be good for anyone else.

Father Lewers assured me that my parents were good people and would come around in time.

"In the meantime, I'm a mess," I said. "Am I wasting my time and money even going through this semester? Either way, I'm not used to being so out of control. I know I have to trust and have faith that everything will turn out, but it's hard to see how anything good can come of this."

It didn't help that the materials Father Lewers had gotten for me didn't really support my case. The words in the 1969 Catholic Bishop's statement on the Catholic Conscientious Objector were not like those I had heard growing up, when church leaders told me what was right or wrong and didn't leave me to ponder or research. I wouldn't have had to wonder whether the Vietnam War was just. Now I was being told that a Catholic "could validly question and abstain from participation in war or the preparations for war."

Could abstain? What happened to moral certitude? What about *should* abstain?

I had spent my life to this point depending on the Church and its leaders. Now, at the most critical time of my moral life, the Church supported my minority position but did not condemn the war. The best the bishops could do was to say that each diocese should provide draft information and counseling. Here I was on the campus of perhaps the most famous Catholic university in the world, and there was no one beyond Father Lewers who could help. Even Father Lewers wasn't sure what to tell me.

All my life I had been faithful to the Catholic Church and its doctrines. I questioned little except my ability to conform and my inability to be perfect. At 24, I didn't smoke or drink. I was still a virgin. All I wanted now was guidance from my Church — and not from the fringe elements or from radical clergy like the Berrigan brothers. Was the war immoral? At least there could be more open dialogue on it at the highest levels, originating in Rome. It was almost as if the hierarchy didn't want to even consider condemning the war, or hadn't done enough research on it to form an opinion. Not every war was the "just war" of Saint Augustine.

The sad truth of it was that if I hadn't received a low lottery number, I probably would have continued on, a good Christian and citizen, supporting a war that was killing perhaps millions. That shame was on me.

I continued my research, torn and conflicted. The Quakers had material about the war and pacifism. Was I a pacifist or simply opposed to *this* war? If everyone could decide which particular war they favored or opposed, how could a country defend itself? I spent hours at the Grotto, usually at night, often lighting a candle. It was quiet and peaceful there. Rather than achieving the desired clarity, the more I researched and reflected the more confused I became.

Meanwhile, to complete my application for Conscientious Objector status, I needed five letters of support from people who could attest to my character, even if they did not oppose the war. Everyone I knew who was in a position to write such a letter probably *did* support the war. I risked losing the respect of all those people.

The responses came quickly. The letter from Father Lewers supported my case: "Let me identify myself by saying that I'm a Roman Catholic priest and am a member of the Law Faculty of the University of Notre Dame … In conclusion, let me state that as a Catholic priest, I'm firmly convinced that Mr. McNicholas is sincere in his statement that he is opposed in conscience to participation in war, and I'm also without hesitation in affirming that his opposition is based upon his religious training and belief."

The other letters were not so successful.

From a monsignor: "Personally, I have mixed feelings in regard to [Conscientious Objector], claims, but I must admit that in many instances my own feelings precede facts and accurate information ... The position he has taken is one that can be reconciled with the teachings of the Catholic Church of which he is a member."

From a former lay college professor: "I must agree that your request is not only rather unusual but also rather surprising and unexpected ... After reading and re-reading your letters several times, I have decided that I cannot, in good conscience, write a letter in support of your request for CO Status ... Finally, your contingent decision to refuse induction if not granted CO status is most disturbing ... I don't recall ever encouraging, either directly, or indirectly through silence, the commission of a felony ... I must advise you against it."

From a Catholic priest: "I must accept Dennis' present decision as a very honest declaration of his conscience, even though I cannot say that I necessarily agree with his position. I emphatically declare that I don't want to go on record as being a protagonist of conscientious objection to war. Such is not the fact."

From another Catholic priest: "I have no doubt about the sincerity and deep feeling of his Conscientious Objector position. I, personally, don't share this posture toward military service with him, nor have I encouraged it."

Needless to say, with scant support from my Church, I was nervous when I appeared before the draft board in Forest Park on October 27, 1970. The layer of smoke that hung in the room reminded me of a pool hall more than of a place where the lives of so many young men were often changed irrevocably.

"Good evening, gentlemen," I said, addressing the panel. The word "evening" was the only word that was true. "As I said in my letter, I'm prepared to serve as a non-combatant medic in a combat platoon."

"Mr. McNicholas," the chairman said, "we are denying your application for Conscientious Objector status and your request to serve as a non-combatant medic in a combat platoon. Do you have any questions?"

I had questions. I had many questions. But if God couldn't answer them, then no one on that panel was likely to, either.

I cleared my throat. "Since you will not allow me to serve as a non-combatant medic, I have a statement to make," I said. "Regardless of your ruling, I am officially withdrawing my application for Conscientious Objector status and will submit to the draft. My application was never intended to avoid or delay my service to my country. However, after much deliberation, I cannot allow someone else to serve and kill or be killed in my place. Good night."

Weeks later, just 10 days before final exams, I received a letter ordering me to report for duty at the same Forest Park facility on December 18, 1971. I turned off the miniature Christmas lights around my window in the Grace Tower dorm, and lay in my bed with the covers pulled up, shivering.

CHAPTER 7

❦

A Case of the Shut-Ups

Exams were coming and I was leaving. It just wasn't right.

I sat in the law school library, thinking. Struggling. So many people were going about their daily routine, talking and laughing, unaware of my predicament. How could they carry on with their normal lives when halfway around the world people our age or younger were dying?

Then it occurred to me that my constitutional-law teacher, Professor Rice, was retired military, having been a lieutenant colonel in the Marine Corps. Maybe he could help.

I went to his office on the second floor and knocked gently on the vintage wooden door with its frosted glass panel.

"Denny, good to see you," said Professor Rice after his secretary showed me in. "What can I do for you?"

I explained my predicament, that I had received orders to report in just a few days with not enough time to finish out the semester.

He pressed down on the intercom. "Mary, can you please get me the Office of the State of Illinois Director of Selective Service?"

Miraculously, a mere fifteen minutes later, the professor had arranged for me to finish out the year before new orders arrived.

As the spring semester began, the remaining weeks of my second year of law school at Notre Dame were much more peace-filled than the preceding months. I tried to prepare for exams. I couldn't adequately explain my decision to be drafted to classmates who knew me well. Most everyone else was consumed with exam preparation. It was also a very difficult and nostalgic time. I looked at the law school seniors, those in their third and final year. Many already had jobs lined up with law firms.

The Dean's Office knew that I'd been drafted and promised that I could return to finish the final year of law school after completing my two years of service. I was struck by how few of the people that I knew, with the exception of Father Lewers, seemed to struggle with the moral dilemma of war that had been consuming me. I was happy to know that I would be able to complete law school eventually, but I felt isolated and full of tumult, Dante descending through the circles of hell.

I spent my last few weeks of freedom back with my family, saying my goodbyes and working out feverishly since I'd be comparatively old among the 18-year-olds in Army basic training. As I approached age 24 I already had pematurely gray hair that didn't help. At least my parents could host a party for me, now that I had saved them the shame of having a cowardly son.

My brother Kevin drove me to the Induction Center on June 16, 1971, one day before my 24th birthday.

ALL YOU WHO ENTER, LET NO HOPE SURVIVE[2]

I entered the Induction Center with only the clothes on my back. Like Alice down the rabbit hole, I disappeared into the bowels of this peculiar, frightening, and potentially life-threatening world.

Hundreds of us gradually filled a large, windowless auditorium. Little if any talking was going on. There was just the exaggerated sound of metal folding chairs being pushed and pulled. The lights were dim, probably for some reason — psychological intimidation?

Then it began. Two men in military dress took the stage.

"On your feet!" said one. "Good morning, my name is Sergeant Russell. Don't any of you ever wear a hat in any of my buildings."

We all stood, even more silent than before.

"You will be tested today to see if you're fit to serve your country," continued the sergeant. "I will make it my personal mission to ensure that you all pass. When I tell you to jump, you'd best jump. I want you up one row at a time, and keep your mouths shut."

He didn't have to tell us twice.

I was in the fifth row, so I had plenty of time to ponder what lay in wait. We were a motley group — height, weight, national origin. So many differences and yet so much in common.

When my row was called, I filed along with the others through a door to the side of the auditorium, where a Sergeant Davis now told us to take off all our clothing except our underpants, put it in a basket, lock the basket, and take the key. "When I call you, take a bottle from that table and go fill it in that room," he said. "I want a bottle of urine from each of you. Fill it up but no topping off. You, yes you, third guy in the second row, wipe that silly-ass grin off your face."

We sat on benches, stripped to our briefs, waiting our turn. A man sitting near me was boasting under his breath to a friend about how he planned to beat the system. "No way in hell I'm goin' in the Army," he said. "I have diabetes."

"No shit," said his friend.

"No, dummy, I have diabetes *today*." He pulled several packets of sugar from the waistband of his BVDs. "Trust me, two of these in the bottle and I'm out of here. Want one?"

I looked away. I was no scientist but even I knew that table sugar wasn't going to present in the urine as diabetes.

Just as in a hospital, in a thin, generic gown, there was a feeling of cold anonymity. Families, net worth, IQ, those things meant nothing. We had been reduced to our lowest common denominator. We were nearly naked, stripped of our dignity, eyes down, hands pressed tightly against our knees. It was as though this position of abject, humble fear were embedded in our DNA, a form of the fetal position.

The Army doctors didn't miss a thing: eyes, ears, every inch. At the last testing station, in a room that was like a small basketball court, we stood on numbered markers on the floor. The door to my right abruptly slammed open. Out came two men dressed in white coats. "Attention. Look at me. Eyes front," said the older of the two men. "Pull down your underpants. Now bend over and grab your ankles."

"This must be the psychological exam," I cracked in a nervous whisper to the recruit on my left, who snickered.

The two men in white coats marched up and down the rows. "Syphilis on three," said one, while the other dutifully took note of it on a clipboard. "Gonorrhea on 11." I looked down at my number on the floor and was relieved to see that it was 17.

The afflicted were directed to get the appropriate shots, but were not excused. They were still expected to serve their country.

"You moron, grab your butt cheeks from the outside, bend over and smile!"

A succession of sergeants swore us in and had us fill out pre-emptive postcards to our loved ones from places we might be stationed: Fort Leavenworth, Kansas; Fort Lewis, Washington; Fort Knox, Kentucky. Every sergeant seemed to feel the need to slam doors on their way either into or out of the room. They all had a serious case of the Shut Up's, too. "Shut up. Who said that? Anybody ask for your opinion?" They said it even if no one had spoken, or had even thought of speaking. "Shut your mouths!"

A door that had just finished slamming slammed again. "Look, a new sergeant," the man to my right whispered. "The other one must be broken."

"Shut up!" the sergeant screamed.

After an insufficient lunch, plus more slamming of doors and various sergeants yelling at us, we were shoved out onto Jackson Boulevard, where two buses were idling. Each beckoned like a praying mantis. We were assigned to a bus and then rode silently, in darkness, most of the night.

A babble of tongues, harsh outcries of despair,
noises of rage and grief, the beating of hands,
and shrill and raucous voices everywhere
all made a mad uproar that never ends,
revolving in that timeless darkened breeze
the way a whirlwind whips the desert sands.[3]

33

CHAPTER 8

❧

Give Me 50

FORT KNOX GOT its start in 1940 and grew in size throughout World War II. By the time I got to there, more than a million trainees had completed its basic-training and other programs, and the Fort was graduating up to 80,000 trainees each year.

I arrived at Fort Knox at 4 a.m., along with a few hundred other recruits from other induction centers. In a field house with an old, dirty smell and an illuminated stage, a drill sergeant screamed at us. "On your feet! My name is Sergeant Rickert. I'm in charge of this phase of your orientation. Now shut up and sit down. I'm going to give you all a gift, because I'm just that kind of guy. I want all of you to be equal in God's eyes and mine as you go forward, so I'm going to give you a 15-minute amnesty. Everyone here who has a weapon, illegal drugs, or anything else you think is stupid, take it to the back of the room and put it in one of the boxes. Ready, go."

More than half the men in the room made a dash to the amnesty area.

The sun was coming up, its faint beams piercing the dirty windows on the east side and heating up the building. The next stop after this metal incubator was the real world of the Army. We were herded to a long building, and amid much shouting and yelling we saw what was in store for us — the barber. Actually, many barbers: non-commissioned officers who manned a row of chairs, in each of which sat a recruit. The recruits sat down with big heads of hair, from crew cuts to Afros, and left with heads that looked like a baby's bottom.

"You're next, beautiful," the drill sergeant said to a flower-child recruit who must have spent years cultivating those flowing blond locks.

34

They almost needed an extra sergeant just to push the broom and clear the floor.

"I wonder if there's anything left to take from us?" I whispered to the guy in front of me.

Needless to say we didn't have the same look when we emerged into the sunlight. We looked like ice cream cones topped with different flavors of ice cream. Also, God does not create all skulls equally, and I was reminded that forceps leave their mark long after their use in the delivery room. There was one recruit named Lester who had a magnificently cratered head, a lunar terrain into which wayward celestial bodies had crashed.

Next, we were marched single-file across a parade ground to another long building. I guessed it was where we would get our clothing, but the combined effect of sleep deprivation with lack of information left me disoriented.

Inside the nondescript, single-story building, a drill sergeant barked at us to strip. "Take your shit off, put it in a box, put your mama's name on it and kiss it good-bye. And keep your mouths shut."

Other drill sergeants, their last names sewn to their left shirt pockets in black letters, shouted out our heights. Each of us was then rewarded with a stack of clothing and shoes. I was even fitted with special new glasses that wrapped around my ears, a design that would enable them to stay on my head when they were located even after an explosion. These glasses were also special, I later realized, because the lenses had been flipped, which caused me massive headaches. "Don't seem to matter much if this stuff fits, does it?" muttered a recruit nearby.

"And I don't see any line for returns," I added.

We left the building out another door, each of us with a duffel bag carrying the rest of our new clothing, having left our old clothing and our identities behind.

Now we were marched to the two-story wooden buildings that would be our sleeping quarters, to the sound of far-off gunfire and the sight of columns of troops marching from nowhere to nowhere. We were told to take a bunk and deposit our duffel bags in the footlockers at the end of the beds. I chose an upper bunk and then sat on one of the footlockers.

"Dennis McNicholas," I said to a man sitting on the lower bunk to my right.

"Lang, Louis," he responded. "You can call me Louie."

I could see that they were mostly kids. I later learned that the average age of the 250 men in my company was just under 18. The average education level was 11.6 years, or just short of high school graduation. Only Louie looked closer to my age — it was June 17, my 24th birthday — and in fact he had finished one year of a two-year program in clinical psychology. His father was a major in the Army.

We were the Third Platoon, Bravo Company, Nineteenth Battalion. We were brought here for the most part by chance, not choice. We were Hispanic, African American, Caucasian. We had one thing in common: regardless of age, education level, skin color, or marital status, we were afraid. There was a war going on. Every night Walter Cronkite reported on the number of American, North Vietnamese and Vietcong troops who had been killed. Within a few short months, each of us would learn numerous ways to kill another human being. We would be expected to act as a unit and to kill in order to protect ourselves, the men we were with, and people we had never met.

How did I get here, I wondered?

There was a commotion at the rear of the barracks. A smaller recruit had tried to impress those around him by hoisting his 100-pound duffel bag, in a move much like a power snatch in weight lifting. With a primal scream, he had attempted to throw the bag over his shoulder. Unfortunately, the laws of physics took over. He got the bag over his shoulder but was unable to stop its trajectory, and now the recruit — I later found out his name was Frank — was lying on the floor on his back.

"Fall out! Formation in the company area! Move! Move!" screamed a drill sergeant. The drill sergeants were ubiquitous and interchangeable. Push-ups were their favored form of punishment, and Frank was subjected to 50 of them right there and then.

"Again!" yelled the drill sergeant when Frank was finished.

"Do you think he'll be able to keep screaming for the entire ten weeks?" whispered Louie beside me.

"Maybe that's his natural voice," I murmured.

The first two weeks of Basic Training were spent learning to minimize the chances we would kill each other or ourselves or, more important, a drill sergeant. It was an awkward and uncomfortable time, kind of like a first date, except that some first dates usually come to a merciful end while this new life kept recurring like in *Groundhog's Day*. There was no escaping from the most awful person you had ever met. Survival depended upon putting up a front, and I was no exception.

For the first time in my life I was stirred deep into the melting pot. My goal was to remain as quiet and private as possible. In some ways, this came naturally to me. My family had never encouraged emotional expression. Feelings were like a fire extinguisher, only to be used in event of emergency. I lay on my back in the upper bunk, unable to sleep. My mother had encouraged us to suffer in silence, just like the saints, and while that training came in handy in the Army, it felt like a form of self-suffocation.

There were real physical effects, too. The genius that designed the toilets had neglected to add stalls, and the toilets were so close that you could touch your neighbor's elbow if you both assumed the throne at the same time. I didn't defecate for two weeks.

We immediately began our weapons training. For most of us this would be the first time we had fired or even held a weapon. (It was a weapon, not a gun. If you called it a gun you did 50 push-ups.)

We marched nearly a mile to the firing range. The closer we got the more anxious I became, and I knew I was not alone. The sound of gunfire grew louder as we rounded the last curve in the road to see hundreds of men lying prone on the ground, firing down-range at paper silhouettes of human bodies spread out at the base of a barren hill. A pall of smoke hung over the tableau, and the smell of spent gunpowder had been gagging us for the last half-mile.

Now it was our turn. The most important thing to remember on the firing range was to keep your weapon pointed up and aimed down-range. I can only say that we were lucky the silhouettes were not firing back that day. The casualties among the recruits would have been devastating.

⌘

June in Fort Knox, Kentucky, can be hot, very hot. In June 1971 the temperatures ran in the nineties every day. Regardless of the weather, we always wore long, olive drab pants, tied off with small elastic bands just above our high-cut black combat boots. We also wore long-sleeved, heavy olive-drab shirts, although we were allowed to roll up the sleeves and could even strip down to our undershirts during Physical Training (PT). The shirts often sported white streaks from the salt we sweated off. The loss of salt was so serious that we were required to take handfuls of salt tablets from a bowl near the end of the chow line, like an after-dinner mint.

On any given day a different drill sergeant led us in PT from a high wooden platform. Few of us were in good shape, and the drill sergeants liked to dispense push-ups with a free hand, like seasonings in a stew.

Soon enough we became acquainted with Master Sergeant Baxter, a 6-foot-7 black man with strikingly broad shoulders and a body that tapered to an unusually trim waist. His wide-brimmed green sergeant's hat cast a shadow on his face, making his moustache even more ominous.

His was a terrifying combination of talents and physical attributes. The rolled-up sleeves of his olive-drab training shirt strained to contain his massive upper arms. The M-16 in his beefy hand looked like a toy. There was a large scar running from the top of his right cheek down to his chin that was rumored to be from a Louisville bar fight. Even the other drill sergeants seemed to shrink before him.

"Gentlemen, push-ups," he screamed at us. "Assume the position. Move it!"

I flopped to the ground in the 100-degree heat. Why did it have to be Baxter on a day like this?

"Give me 50!" shouted Baxter. I don't know why his arithmetic was so bad. He always asked for 50 when he really meant twice that.

"Check out Lester," Dan muttered next to me. Dan was another college grad, whose home was in Elmhurst, Illinois. "I think he's our lowest common denominator."

Lester Lampley with the cratered head looked ashen. His arms were visibly trembling and we were barely into the first dozen push-ups. Lester, 18 years old and just under 6 feet tall, had been born on a mountaintop in Tennessee, just like Davy Crockett. That's where the comparison ended, because Lester was no Davy Crockett. The physical and mental demands of Basic Training were too much for him.

We finally finished but knew we had to wait for the command to stand up. We hovered in the push-up position, slowly dying. These days people pay good money for yoga classes where they willingly hold this plank position, but back then we had no idea we were onto a trend.

"Okay, you pussies!" Baxter shouted. "Nobody gets up until everybody has their knees off the ground and backs straight."

Baxter was smiling. This made him happy.

We were all exhausted. We started looking around to see who among us was holding up the works. The sweat dripping from my forehead was forming a circle of mud beneath me.

"Lester, you mother f*****!" Baxter screamed, finding the culprit. "Get your sorry ass off the ground and into position or I swear you'll never have children."

Lester finally got with the program, but our misery wasn't over. Neither was his. They followed up PT with what was known as a close-order drill, a grueling double-header for a hot day.

Perhaps because of what had happened at birth to his head, Lester suffered with the whole left-right orientation. He often had to guess which direction he was supposed to turn when a particular order was given.

On this day, he quickly guessed wrong.

"What the f*** do you think you're doing, Lampley?" shouted Sergeant Baxter. "You best get yo' head out of yo' ass, boy! Drop and give me 50."

The fate of any recruit who violated a command during close-order drill was to perform 50 push-ups with his M-16 balanced atop his hands so that it didn't touch the ground. Lester's weapon immediately touched the dirt, and I thought Sergeant Baxter would have a coronary. "You're a stupid mother!" he screamed. "See this? Take this rock and put it in your left hand. When I say left, go with the rock. And drop down and give me another 50."

No sooner would Lester finish his 50 push-ups and jump back in line with his rifle over his right shoulder and rock in his left hand than Sergeant Baxter would bark out another command and Lester would get it wrong.

"Halt!" screamed Baxter. "I said HALT!" But Lester's neocortex was no longer sending messages to his lower extremities. "Drop and give me another 50!"

I'm sure that to this day, Lester Lampley holds the record for the most push-ups ever done at Fort Knox.

A month into Basic Training, Captain Jimmy Barnes, Commander of Company B, Nineteenth Battalion, was ready to see his Bravo Company pass by the company headquarters. The drill sergeants felt we were ready, too. Well, some of them did.

By now I had risen to Platoon Guide, with three stripes on my arm. I was expected to help pull this off.

It was important to look good in front of Captain Jimmy Barnes. (I think I can call him Jimmy by now without fear of punishment.) He was a soldier's soldier. His khaki pants were always starched and creased, no matter the temperature or time of day. He had a dark tan and maybe two percent body fat. He had already served in Vietnam. On his head was a helmet liner with two silver bars reflecting his position in life with respect to the subhuman forms that served under him. His silver-coated sunglasses allowed him to see you, but not vice versa. He had a unique talent whereby he could have a cigarette between his lips on one side and a toothpick on the other, and somehow manage to switch their positions without using a hand.

"Relax, Lester," I said to the one recruit who could really gum up the works for all of us. "You'll do fine." I hoped to convince both of us.

Lester's diet hadn't improved much since he was drafted. He still looked gaunt, perhaps 155 pounds. His shorn blond hair looked like peach fuzz on a misshapen peach.

"I think I can do it," he said, sweating profusely and pushing his glasses back up his long nose.

Our platoon would be the third to pass in front of Captain Barnes, giving him plenty of material for comparison. I watched Drill Sergeants Callen and Versted, who were in charge of us, but couldn't tell how either of them felt about our coming out, so to speak, and performing in front of Captain Barnes. Either way it would be a reflection on them.

All five platoons were lined up in columns of two, all of us wearing the metal helmets that were designed to reduce the speed of bullets and shrapnel on their way through our skulls. We also wore canvas belts to hold our canteens and bayonets, and carried a rifle on our right shoulder. We stood quietly at "parade rest," awaiting further directions.

"Attention!" barked Sergeant Callen. "Eyes front and shut up. Let's get this right. Forward march."

Lester's problem processing marching orders revealed itself four steps into our march. He was focusing on the feet of the man in front of him so as to stay in step, but it didn't work. He hopped to try to get back in step, and when he hopped his canteen banged loudly against his belt. His glasses slid off the bridge of his nose. His helmet lifted off his head and crashed down again. Lester's gait didn't affect the men ahead of him, but was a disaster for those behind him who were trying to keep in step. When Lester hopped, all the soldiers behind him hopped. No sooner had Lester hit the ground than he would find himself out of step and hop again.

On that glorious day, the Third Platoon marched in hippety-hop fashion across the company grounds in full view of Captain Jimmy Barnes, who I am sure is still suffering from post-traumatic stress.

CHAPTER 9

Straw Men

There at the summit two small fires burned
  and another signaled back from far away,
    so distant it could barely be discerned.
I turned to the sea of all wisdom: "What does it say,
    that flame? And what is meant by the answering light?
    And the ones who lit these fires, who are they?"[4]

FRIDAY NIGHT, WEEK Four. The war raged on. Each day brought us closer to the inevitability of our final orders and permanent assignments. As American troops were withdrawn to the cities, especially Saigon, increasing numbers of military police were sent to those locations to maintain order and provide security.

While most of the men of the Third Platoon were in Louisville, anaesthetizing themselves in the bars or the brothels, I was on the front steps of the wooden barracks, polishing my boots. Carole King ruled the airways, and "It's too late baby …" played on somebody's lonely radio.

"What's up, Denny?" It was Dan Slane, another of the few college graduates in our company. We had matching outfits on: baggy olive-drab pants, white T-shirts, and of course our double dog tags. They were doubled so that if you died in combat, one could be taken so an accurate body count could be made, with the other left behind for identifying the corpse, especially if there was nothing left of the face.

"Hey, Dan. I decided to bring excitement to my Friday night by polishing my second pair of boots," I said. "Then I plan to get really crazy, let my hair down and clean my M-16."

"Cool, I'll join you." Dan went to fetch his boots and his rifle. "So how's your day been?"

I sighed. "Every day is a challenge," I said. "I was ordered to send George Johnson down to Company Headquarters, and George said that if this was a set-up he'd come back and kick my ass. Then while we were down in the pits doing hand-to-hand combat, Bill Smith got in my face and said he should have had my job of Platoon Guide. These people are supposed to be on our side. Dan, let me ask you, do you ever feel isolated, like you don't fit in?"

"All the time," he replied.

"I mean, we can't help that we were drafted, or that we happen to be as old as or older than many of the sergeants and officers."

"Yeah, it's strange taking orders from some of them."

"Sergeant McCoy really has it in for me. I'd like to rip those three stripes off his arm and that silly moustache off his lip."

We polished our boots for a while in silence.

"You know," I said, "before this place I was able to remove myself from the source of my anger. Now I feel trapped. How angry will we be when someone's actually trying to kill us?"

"Whoa, want to go down to the parade grounds and bayonet some straw dummies?"

"Nah. But you know that anywhere but here we would never put up with this crap. It's one thing for them to train us, but why do they have to abuse and humiliate us? I won't be in long enough to ever have any more authority than Platoon Guide. I only took this job to help recruits learn how to stay alive and in turn help me stay alive, too."

Dan stood and stretched. "Well, I'm done for the night," he said. "No one should have this much fun."

❡

On Saturday afternoons they posted the following week's training schedule on the bulletin board near the front door of the barracks. A typical week might involve hand grenades, bayonets, training on the M-50 machine gun, grenade launchers, map reading, "pugil" sticks, hand-to-hand combat, or administering first aid.

"Oh, shit," said Hector Martinez when he read the schedule preceding the seventh week of our eight-week training. "We get gassed Monday."

The most hated event of Basic Training was when they put you in a gas chamber and had you take off your gasmask and breathe in a mouthful of ortho-chlorbenzylidenedimalonitrile, the active substance in CS gas, or tear gas. Ostensibly, the exercise is to give you confidence in your gear, but most of us saw it as an unnecessary rite of passage.

"Uh-oh," I said. "Sergeant Haynes hates me. He'll make me stay in there forever."

"Sergeant Picket hates me, too. They both served a tour in Vietnam, got their three stripes, and now as buck sergeants they want to take it out on us."

"Yeah, they're both around 21 years old. They especially seem to like screwing with the older guys, and that would be me."

After all the platoons had reported on Monday, Sergeant Callen addressed the troops. "If you haven't manned up yet, today's your day," he said.

I thought I *had* manned up by now, but perhaps I was wrong.

Once tear gas gets you, your eyes water and you lose the ability to see clearly. It also turns you into a personal saliva-manufacturing plant, sending it dripping from the nose and mouth like a fountain.

Several minutes into the experience inside the chamber, where the gas was billowing from a canister in the center, the ten of us in our group were ordered to remove our masks and breathe deep, like we were at a refreshing spa. Sergeant Haynes got to keep his mask on as we stood toe-to-toe and he yelled at me to breathe in. I did as told, but apparently I hadn't taken a deep enough quaff of the noxious gas.

"Breathe in again, you son of a bitch!" he screamed.

Normally, recruits take one breath and are allowed to dash for the door, staggering into the sunlight they still cannot see, but Sergeant Haynes made me take three breaths until he released me. Filled with rage, I would have loved to tear off his mask and practice some of that hand-to-hand combat I'd been taught, but there was a policy against attacking non-commissioned officers.

Outside the chamber, we were like chickens without heads, stumbling around, unable to see our hands as they groped like sea anemones searching for purchase.

It took half an hour to recover from the effects of the gas. I knew it would take longer than that to cope with my horror of how easy it had been to dislike a fellow human being — one that ostensibly was on my side.

"O you who show such wild hostility,
attacking him with bestial violence,
tell me why," I said...[5]

The pace of our training picked up as we approached the end of our eight-week training. The heightened pace and accompanying exhaustion had a way of numbing the senses, like an Army-authorized narcotic. Even the drill sergeants, who never had any trouble getting in touch with their anger, had a sense of urgency and purpose about them as they tried to cram in all the teaching they could. Any one lesson might mean the difference between life and death.

"Third Platoon, report," Sergeant Clayton shouted.

"All present or accounted for, Sergeant," I shouted back.

"Okay, shut up. In case you didn't read the schedule, today we do bayonet training. Sergeant Baxter will be your instructor."

My glasses were already fogged from the heat and humidity on this hot August morning. I heard mumbling and realized it was George Johnson, a short, skinny guy with a triple-X attitude. Some say that the military can help you turn your life around and make a man out of you. George must have missed that sales pitch during orientation.

"George, keep your mouth shut," I hissed. "We'll all get in trouble."

George wasn't much for protocol. "I don't need to mess with no silly-ass bayonets," he said. "I'm just gonna shoot those mothers."

45

"Fine, George. Why don't you tell Sergeant Baxter that your combat knowledge and depth of experience make it unnecessary for you to partake of a lesson on how to use a bayonet? I'm sure he'll understand. Meanwhile, shut up or I can have Sergeant Callen pull you out for some early PT."

George took his hat off and moved toward me. Before he got any closer Sergeant Callen approached us from behind. "Any trouble here, McNicholas?"

"No, drill sergeant. George just asked if his hat was on straight."

"Cut the crap and get ready. You're next."

Bayonet instruction was held in a field with a 10-by-10-foot wooden stand some six feet off the ground. We spread out across the field in formation with the sun directly in our eyes. Sergeant Baxter mounted the platform and the sun behind him formed a nimbus, making him look larger and more threatening than usual.

"Today I will teach you the fine art of bayonet warfare," he said. "This is war up close and personal. This is war so close you can smell the enemy and see the sweat on his forehead. If you're good, you'll live. If the other guy is better, you'll die." He held up his bayonet-tipped M-16 in his right hand. The edge of the bayonet glinted in the sun. "This weapon is not designed to wound a man. When used properly, it will leave your opponent dead. And that's what you want, because a wounded soldier is a dangerous enemy."

We paired up, spread out, and practiced pretending to kill each other. We learned to parry and thrust, feint and spin. "I want to hear you, too. I want you to scream so loud they can hear you back at company headquarters."

After forty minutes of parrying and thrusting, feinting and spinning, and screaming our heads off, we were reunited with Sergeant Callen, who pointed us downfield to a bunch of dummies filled with straw. "I want to hear some noise. I want you to charge down there, four at a time, and stab those dummies at least four times. Then get out of the way, because the next four won't be far behind you. You don't want them to mistake you for a dummy."

The younger recruits treated this like football practice. Almost everyone seemed oblivious to the implications, that we had just learned a new way of killing another human being. But, no matter what I thought about the drill sergeants, I knew that if I were in combat in Vietnam in a darkened jungle there was no one I would rather have with me than Sergeant Baxter, holding his bayonet-tipped M-16 and screaming orders at full blast.

♋

We began Basic Training on June 28, 1971, and were graduated eight weeks later, on August 20, 1971. Only then did we find out where we would do our AIT, Advanced Individual Training.

"I heard Sergeant Callen talking to Sergeant Versted," said Louie. "He said he expects at least half of the platoon will get orders for Fort Polk. He said Polk was the doorway to Vietnam."

I had always known that Fort Polk was a possibility for me. It was a possibility for anyone.

Finally, they assembled us in the company area.

"Heads up," Sergeant Baxter yelled. "Let's get this over with. You're getting your orders. After you do, go back and finish packing. You'll be transported from Fort Knox tomorrow. Assemble on the parade grounds at 8 a.m. tomorrow. Sergeants, start distributing the orders."

Sergeants Callen and Versted moved quietly through our ranks, handing out all 50 orders. Louie arrived at his bunk only minutes after I did, and Dan wasn't far behind.

"What's the verdict?" I asked.

Dan spoke up first. "Fort Benjamin Harrison in Indianapolis for me," he said.

"Me too," said Louie. "Clerical and administrative AIT. Fort Harrison, here I come!"

47

"This is where we part ways," I said. "I've got orders for Fort Gordon, Georgia. Military Police School."

We said our goodbyes at the buses the next morning and gathered with our new groups. From where I was I could see the boys who'd be going to Fort Polk. Most of them were only 18 years old. I had no wish to join them, but was struck by the apparent unfairness of the system. All these boys really had to know was how to assemble and disassemble an M-16 in the dark, but because most of them had no real formal education, they weren't qualified for the kind of advanced training I'd be getting. As a consequence, they would now be the fodder of the war. The drill sergeants might have been rougher on the older guys and the college-educated ones, but now these younger ones sat in silence looking at the ground or tying and retying their duffle bag straps. Gone were the dreams of conquest they'd had when they screamed out their bravery at a bunch of straw dummies.

My eyes were drawn to one solider in particular. He sat quietly, alone, no primal screams or chest thumping. His helmet lay between his feet, boots loosely laced, hands cupping his head as if to hold it up. I moved closer, as if drawn by his pain. I was close enough to see his tears as they fell, striking his helmet.

> Here tears themselves make tears impossible.
>   The grief is blocked, turning inward when it tries
>   to express itself, making pain more painful still,
> for knots are formed by the first tears each soul cries,
>   resembling a crystal visor as they spread
>   to fill the hollows that surround the eyes.[6]

CHAPTER 10

Bunkmates

THE ELATION WITH which I received the news that I was not being shipped off to Fort Polk was short-lived. I couldn't sleep as my bus traveled through the night, rain streaking the windows.

Fort Gordon, the training facility for the Army and Marine Corps military policemen, was named after Confederate Lieutenant General John Brown Gordon. My bus arrived at the outskirts of Augusta, Georgia, at about 5 a.m.

"I don't think I slept at all last night," I said to the man standing closest to me.

"No one did," he said. He was coughing and slapping clouds of dust from his shirt. "I've heard of the red clay of Georgia, but this is ridiculous!"

"Dennis McNicholas," I said, offering him a hand. "Chicago."

"Pat Murphy, Cleveland," he said. "Sure you're in the right place? Your hair, it's gray."

"Premature, on my mother's side."

If anything, Pat looked older than I was. He stood about 6-foot-2 and had a beat-up look, as if he had boxed in his youth. "Were you on the same bus?" I asked him. "I didn't see you."

"I was sitting in back. Sometimes I like to be alone."

The dust billowed with every recruit stepping off the bus. In the fields to our left the moisture-laden air formed a ground fog some four feet high. "I can't make out a thing," I said.

"How did you end up here?" he asked.

"Low lottery number. I was drafted in the middle of my second year of law school."

"Guess what? I was in law, too! I was on the verge of graduating. I finished all but one class at John Carroll Law School."

"Really? But ... when were you born?"

"November 18, 1940."

"Pat, the draft was only for men born between 1944 and 1950."

"I enlisted."

I surely did not know what to make of this guy. There was a war raging in Southeast Asia and young men were dying every day, yet here was someone who could have avoided serving altogether, or at least gone in as an officer, and still decided to enlist.

As the red sun continued to struggle up from the heavy moist air, more buses arrived to transport us to the base. Thanks to the Army's penchant for alphabetizing everything, Dennis McNicholas and Pat Murphy were often thrown together over the course of our time at Fort Gordon.

At least the barracks here were more modern, not like the firetraps at Fort Knox. These newer barracks were of corrugated metal stretched in a half-moon shape over a concrete slab. It reminded me of a long barbecue grill that would cook us thoroughly, as long as we turned ourselves over occasionally.

Pat and I were assigned to the same barracks. "Want to bunk together?" I asked him.

"That's my first and best offer. Sure," he said.

At our new living area, we threw our duffel bags on the floor. Pat chose the bottom bunk. "Say, did you notice these guys aren't much older than the ones we left in basic training?" he asked.

"You're right," I said. "They'll be such young policemen. Strange, isn't it? In law school we were being trained to defend the people we will now be trained to arrest."

"Maybe it will give us a better perspective."

We got to know each other much better as the weeks passed. The best time for us to talk was while we were lying in our bunks; otherwise Pat often seemed distracted and would look up and away when we spoke.

The training at Fort Gordon was much like that at Fort Knox, but with less emphasis on PT. We still had drill sergeants teaching us, but we trained with different weapons. The primary weapon of an infantryman was the lightweight M-16. Now we trained with grenade launchers, .50-caliber machineguns, and the 45-caliber handgun that was the principal weapon of an MP. We also spent a lot of time in class studying military law.

Pat and I spent a lot of our free time together. We went to the library and to church. Sometimes we went to the sawdust pits to practice hand-to-hand combat. Each night we ran two laps of the mile-long oval road that fronted the barracks, sprinting the last lap. We often talked from our bunks at night after lights-out.

Pat was a war baby, born in Cleveland on November 18, 1940. He was one of three children. His mother was born near Galway, and his father was from Sligo, also in Ireland. He said his mother had a way of predicting strange things that in many cases actually came to pass.

Pat had excelled in his grammar school years, though not quite as much during high school. Because they were a family of modest means, the children had to work their way through college; it took Pat five years to get his undergraduate degree. He then entered an evening law school program that allowed him to work full-time during the day.

"Why did you drop out of law school?" I asked. "I don't get it."

"Got bored. Wanted to do something else," he said. "I was one class short of graduation and became a claims adjustor for an insurance company instead."

"Why in the world you would volunteer to fight in this war?"

"I wanted a change of pace. Thought the Army would be good for me."

"I'm as patriotic as the next man, but this war is confusing. I wish I'd been drafted during WWII."

"Dennis, me boy, I never think much about all that."

"In case you hadn't noticed, this war isn't very popular. No one will be lining the streets and cheering us when we get back, if we get back. Speaking of which, how are you about the prospect of going to Vietnam?"

"Sorry, what's that again? My mind drifted."

"Pat, pay attention. This is important. In a very few weeks you and I will find out whether we're going into harm's way. We could get killed. We might kill other people. Even if we don't die, we might get messed up. Am I getting through to you? I don't want to shoot someone and I sure as hell don't want to get shot. Doesn't any of this bother you?"

"Huh, I hadn't thought about it," he said. "I've never been to Vietnam. Kind of like to see the place."

How could someone with Pat's intelligence not even think about the consequences here?

We were silent. After a while, I thought Pat must have fallen asleep, but then he said, quite calmly, "Dennis, I saw Mary, the Blessed Mother, earlier today."

"Excuse me?" I said, startled. I hoped he was kidding. "What did she say?" I asked with a laugh.

"Dennis, me boy, she didn't say anything. She didn't have to."

I stared at the ceiling for a long time, trying to make sense of Pat Murphy.

༒

On graduation day at Fort Gordon, the Army had one last chance to line us up in alphabetical order. Two smartly dressed drill sergeants moved down the row. One carried a clipboard, the other a box of glass bottles. Everyone who'd been assigned to Vietnam had to give a urine sample prior to being shipped out. This was the moment when we would find out: Getting a bottle was bad. Anything else would be a relief.

I leaned slightly forward to see Pat, seven men to my right. "Yo, Pat, good luck!" I stage-whispered.

"Thanks!" he boomed in a voice that could be heard from Allen to Yarrow. "You too, Dennis!"

"Shut the f*** up!" screamed Drill Sergeant Considine. "Eyes front. I'll get to you soon enough."

We would just have to wait for our orders. Most of us knew the odds.

"Donovan, bottle. Duffy, bottle," said Sergeant Considine as he moved down the line. "Latine, bottle. Lawrence, bottle." He was now only eight men to my left. I was having trouble focusing on the words coming from his mouth.

Steve Lieberman, standing not far to my left, turned toward me anxiously. "Riding around Saigon in an open Jeep doing night curfew with white MP letters on my helmet and sleeve won't attract the attention of a sniper," he whispered. "What could possibly go wrong?"

Tom McDaniel was the last man between the sergeant and me. "Eyes front! Shut up!" said Sergeant Considine. "McDaniel, bottle."

Now it was my turn. The sergeant looked at me, handed me a sheet of paper with my orders, and moved on without saying a word. No bottle.

I could have kissed the ground, but I stood ramrod straight, still afraid to breathe in case the sergeant changed his mind and came back to tell me it was all a horrible joke.

He didn't come back. He continued moving down the line.

"Murphy, bottle." My heart sank as the sergeant handed Pat a bottle. I stole a look at him, but Pat was still standing tall, eyes front, a smile on his face, gently rocking front to back and seemingly unfazed.

CHAPTER 11

The Rocket Ranch

I'D BEEN ORDERED to Arlington, Illinois. I'd never heard of it, so I double-checked with Sergeant Tyler. "That's Arlington Heights, Illinois, assigned to the 45th Air Defense Brigade," he told me.

I was confused. There was a large shopping center near Arlington Heights but I didn't know that a brigade was needed to protect it. Christmas shopping must have gotten more aggressive since I was drafted.

Pat and I shared a cab to the airport in Louisville. We didn't talk much on the way, and there were no hugs at the terminal.

"Good luck, Pat."

"Good luck to you too, Dennis."

There was so much left unspoken. Neither of us even thought about how we might stay in touch. That was that after eight weeks together, bonded to the same goal. We went our separate ways, left alone with our own thoughts.

I reported for duty at the headquarters of the 45th Air Defense Brigade in Arlington Heights, Illinois, after a one-week leave at home. It was late October 1971.

The brigade consisted of 145 nuclear missile sites stretching from Milwaukee to Detroit. This system was created in the mid-to-late 1950s to counter what was believed to be a serious threat posed by Soviet strategic bombers. Each of the sites was armed with long-range Nike Hercules nuclear missiles. There were an estimated 3000 nuclear warheads in the brigade, with yields of 2, 20, and 30 kilotons.

After two weeks at the Arlington Heights site, I was transferred to the Nike base in Porter, Indiana. We called it the Porter Rocket Ranch.

"Private McNicholas reporting for duty," I said while saluting smartly.

"At ease, McNicholas," said Captain Milton, the base commander. Along with nearly every other officer on base, he was younger than I was. "We've been expecting you. I see you were transferred here to become part of the MP unit. Take your gear down to the first barracks on the right adjoining the perimeter road and see Sergeant Kincaid. He'll help you get settled. Fall out at 6 a.m. tomorrow for inspection and get acclimated. Any questions?"

The interior of the barracks was lined with bunk beds. Privacy, it seemed, was still limited to civilians. I set out to find Sergeant Kincaid.

"Find an empty bunk, McNicholas," he said. "The MPs all report to me. You'll be on duty for 24 hours and off for at least 24. You'll pull guard duty at the launch area located 1.5 miles east of this location. Welcome to the Porter Rocket Ranch."

Our missile installation, based upon its location, was on 15-minute status, 24 hours a day, seven days a week. This meant that we had to be ready to launch missiles within 15 minutes of receiving an order, so the MPs and other personnel were required to remain clothed for their entire 24-hour shift.

It took several shifts to get acclimated, especially the part where you stay up all night in a small structure with little or no lighting. The flies and mosquitoes, too, took some getting used to.

Within the Launch Area was another area enclosed by a high fence topped with concertina wire. The underground missiles were located within this area. In all there were four underground elevators, each holding one missile ready for launching. The theory was that we would not get much advance warning.

The combat exercises were quite impressive. Loud sirens bellowed out a warning as the silo doors opened. As each elevator rose, the launcher was raised in such a way that the missile was pointed skyward and ready for launching as soon as the elevator reached ground level.

I soon came to understand why the Battery Control Area was located so far from the Launch Area. In the event of an accidental detonation of a missile in the Launch Area, everyone at the Battery Control Area would have time to bend over and kiss their asses good bye.

Some three months after my tour began we had war games. At the Launch Area this meant periodically wearing gas masks and rain ponchos. The theory was that the poncho would slow down the absorption by our bodies of the effects of nuclear fallout. It was the belief of the Army that the Russians would target us before we tried to destroy their bombers.

We assembled in the bomb shelter for instructions. "Okay, men, heads up," said Sergeant Jones. "What I have to tell you may save your life and mine some day."

To better understand why his message was compelling, I should explain that the Launch Area with its nuclear missiles was bounded on several sides by residential neighborhoods. It wasn't uncommon for me to be stationed at the main gate with a loaded .45-caliber handgun, the standard weapon for MPs, just thirty feet from a yellow school bus unloading fifth graders.

Sergeant Jones continued. "In the event we are attacked, you will only live if you quickly move to this shelter and get hosed down in the outer room to shed any radioactive particles from your poncho and boots. Look around you. What do you see? I'll tell you what you see. You see a small concrete building with space only for those on this site. Those people across the street are going to try to get inside MY building! I don't want those people inside MY building! You don't want those people inside of MY building! If we are to carry out our mission, those people cannot gain access to this area. If they try to climb the fences, your job is to keep them out. We cannot carry out our mission with civilians in the way. Listen to what I am saying! We cannot carry on our mission if you are dead. Do I make myself clear?"

As a member of the Military Police unit charged with protecting the Launch Site, I felt the need to ask a question.

"Sergeant."

"McNicholas?"

"Yes, Sergeant. How do you propose we keep the civilians out of the compound if we're under nuclear attack?"

The Sergeant didn't bat an eye. "You do whatever American fighting men have been doing for over two hundred years. You improvise and get the job done."

But look to the valley. All who interfere
with others by violence, doing them injury,
are boiled in the river of blood that is coming near.[7]

CHAPTER 12

⁕

The Best Blind
Date Ever

In January 1973, my good grammar school friend Tom called me while I was on my parents' couch watching the TV series *Emergency*, like any socially inept young man on a Saturday afternoon. I often drove home when I had at least two days off.

"Listen," said Tom. "Terri and I know a great girl, Karin — that's K-a-r-i-n. Beautiful, intelligent, a social worker, and pro-life. You'll have a lot in common. Want to double-date tonight?"

"Let me check my social calendar."

"Hah. We'll pick you up around seven."

I was really excited. Tom was a good friend and I trusted him. I asked my mom how to turn on the iron.

Tom called again around five o'clock. Karin had made up with her ex-boyfriend and the double date was called off. Back to the TV.

In April I participated in an Army program that allowed me to work for a law firm for several months before my discharge in order to ease the transition to civilian life.

On a warm Saturday afternoon in May, I had just come back from a long run, a towel draped over my shoulders, Tom called again. "Remember Karin and that almost-date back in January?" he asked.

"Can't say that I do," I said. "There are so many almost-dates to keep track of."

"She broke up with that boyfriend again, wise guy."

Terri and Tom picked me up at 7 p.m., and we drove to get Karin from where she was spending the weekend with her parents at their home in Rolling Meadows. "When you meet her, call her Kari," Terri instructed me.

When we picked up Kari, I met her parents, Bob and Fran, and her grandmother. Then the double-daters went off to The Barn, a restaurant known for the bottomless baskets of peanuts on each table. The broken pieces and partial nuts were thrown on the floor to make room for the new supply, lending The Barn a distinct aroma and a crunching sound as patrons and staff moved from place to place.

We were seated at a round table. Terri and Kari were best friends, so at first I mostly listened until I relaxed enough to contribute a bit to the conversation. Suddenly I found myself speaking — not just the usual small talk, but about feelings I normally would have shared only with family and the closest friends, if at all.

"Kari, I have to be honest with you," I said. "Something has been bothering me." I could tell from her reaction that she expected the worst. "I felt uncomfortable that even though your grandmother was in the room with us, none of our conversation was directed to her."

Kari's shoulders relaxed and the smile returned to her face. I later learned that she and her grandmother had a strong emotional bond.

It was a good start, and certainly the best date I'd ever had. The next weekend all four of us attended the Renaissance Fair in Wisconsin. That's when I learned that Kari and Terri were about to spend the summer in Israel working on a kibbutz.

I felt like a starving man. We had until Kari's plane departed on June 20, so we spent every day together. Kari was like a sculpture that revealed something beautiful and deeply interesting from every new angle.

A few days before Kari's trip, I walked out of the gates of Porter Rocket Ranch, having concluded my two-year tour of duty. My banishment there had turned out to be a blessing in disguise. The missile base was located only 50 miles from South Bend, Indiana, and the dean of my old law school had allowed me to take classes during my 24-hour layovers. By the time I passed through the concertina-wire-topped gate for the last time, on June 16, 1973, I had managed to complete one semester of my third year of law school — all while serving full-time in the Army.

As I passed through the wormhole back into the free world, it occurred to me that I had done nothing special to merit assignment to Arlington Heights and then to Porter while so many others I knew had been sent into the cross-hairs of Vietnam. There had been no intervention by some special person or politician. In so many ways it didn't make sense.

I drove to the headquarters of the 45th Air Defense Brigade in Arlington Heights for my final processing, and then straight to Kari. I had so much to tell her. We went to a local restaurant and found a quiet booth.

"Tom tells me you are and have been opposed to the war," I said. "Kari, I want to share as much as I can with you about who I am before you leave so we don't spend our summer dreaming about a future that will never be."

"I agree," she said. "But what terrible thing do you need to tell me? What's bothering you?"

"Although I just finished my two years in the Army, I don't want you to think I'm some kind of warrior. Actually, I had applied for conscientious-objector status and was rejected. Maybe Tom already told you."

"He didn't."

"Let me say this first. Even in the most intense training, learning to kill with bayonets, I came to realize that most of us were not training to defend democracy or our country, or for any of the reasons the politicians tell us. It wasn't about defeating Communism. It was about staying alive and coming home. It was then that I was reminded why I had agreed to enter the military after abandoning my conscientious-objector application. If I hadn't, someone else would have taken my place and faced the same fears and risks, perhaps even lost his life. My actions, or inaction, might have resulted in the death of a fellow human being anyway. So I did what I thought was right."

Kari smiled wryly. "In case you're wondering, this does not diminish my feelings for you."

"There's more to the story."

I told her about some of the letters that ostensibly had supported my bid for conscientious-objector status but in fact had undermined it. "Looking back now, I know I was naïve," I said. "I had spent my life to that point looking to my parents, my church, and my priests to tell me what was right and wrong. The letters did not give me clarity. The opposite, in fact. The church supported my position yet distanced itself from condemning the war. The bishops' proclamation in 1969 was in any case too little, too late. We'd been in the war over eight years at that point. So, 'Thou shalt not lie' is an absolute, but 'Thou shalt not kill' was entirely up to me. It made me confused."

It was refreshing and cathartic to share this with someone else. I felt I had really kept it inside all this time, bottling it up while the bottle kept getting shaken.

Kari then shared her own feelings about the war. She was opposed, and had been for years. "For me, it was the ceaseless barbarity of a struggle that had gone on for so long with no clear rationale," she said. "I've marched for peace and for an end to this war. Our involvement has been foolish and imprudent. I wish the church were more vocal on the subject of the morality of the war. I haven't thought about this as much as you, but I stay on in the church even though the war and other issues bother me. For example, why are there no female priests? I stay on because I want to fight for changes that I believe are critical like St. Francis who worked to rebuild the church from within. I'm often confused and angry, but I won't leave the church."

Another layer had been peeled back. I was more in love than before.

There had been a time when I could barely open my mouth around a woman, and now the conversation flowed. "People have gathered in groups to worship something, animate or inanimate, for most of recorded history," I said. "Like people fending off the cold, I think we gather for spiritual warmth. The Catholic Church is not just the church of the Pope, the cardinals, or the bishops. It is also the church of those who stay on. I'll be damned if I'll be chased off by anyone who sins and tries to take my church from me. After all, I'm a sinner too. The people here in my church community who stay on are my faith family. They show up when children are born and receive their sacraments. They show up to celebrate what brings us together. They show up to heal the sick and console those left behind. We depend on each other. I refuse to travel around looking for a church that's just right for me."

"I know what you mean," said Kari. "My faith and church mean everything to me. I don't know how people live without faith, without a belief in God."

"Those are exactly my feelings. I stay on because I choose to stay on. I want to fight for changes that I believe are critical. Kari, these several weeks have given me hope. For so long I felt I would never find someone who would accept me."

"Me too! I've gone down so many romantic dead ends that I was beginning to feel there wasn't anyone for me here. It got so bad that I thought about leaving Illinois and becoming a lay volunteer in Alaska."

"Please tell me you're not coming back from Israel and then going straight off to Alaska," I said. "I can't wait all summer and then have to say goodbye to you again."

I had never felt so safe and natural with a woman in my entire adult life. With Kari, I never felt judged. For her part, she said she felt the same, that she could be her real self with me "and not like I'm in a debate, defending myself and hoping to emerge the victor."

I proposed to Kari on December 22, right after my final exam for law school, in a park that is now just one block from the home we have shared for decades.

CHAPTER 13

❦

Accepting the Charges

KARI AND I were married in the summer of 1974.

We both worked full time, and spent Saturdays with family and at church, and Sundays sleeping in and being with each other.

We looked forward to having children. We decided to call the first baby we were going to have "Mario" until the child's birth. On March 1, 1975, after a pregnancy test, Kari called me at work to tell me that Mario would be joining us for dinner that night.

We were over the moon. We bought baby books and went through lists of baby names, but Kari began spotting early in the third month. We lost Mario three weeks later.

After Kari's surgery, when she was settled in her room, I tried to comfort her, but we were both disconsolate. After about an hour I went to the cafeteria for a quick dinner. Upon returning, I found Kari with her face buried in her hands. Our pastor, Father Warner, had been to see her, and had left her sobbing.

"I can't believe him, that bastard! I'll never forgive him," she said through her tears. "Do you know what he told me? He said that some people were just not meant to be parents."

"Oh, Kari."

"What is God trying to tell me? Does this mean we can't have children?"

"I'm sure that God isn't telling us we shouldn't be parents," I said. "I don't know what the message is, but I know it isn't going to come from Father Warner. Don't listen to him. We both know so many good priests like my uncle and Father Dillon."

Kari's physical recovery took several days. The emotional recovery took longer, but we tried again, and became pregnant for a second time.

This time we were more anxious, and tried in feeble ways to protect each other. It didn't work. Within six months of the first miscarriage we lost another baby, while Father Warner's cruel message continued to play in our heads on an endless loop. One Sunday morning, when our doubts were at their worst, a phone call startled me from a deep sleep. I struggled to find the receiver.

"Hello, who is it?"

"This is the operator. I have a collect call for Dennis from Patrick Murphy. Will you accept the charges?"

"Of course, operator. Pat, where are you? *How* are you?"

"I just left church," he said. "I had to leave early. I didn't like the looks of some of the people. I stopped at a pay phone. I'm a little confused today."

"Pat, where are you living?"

"I live in a halfway house. I'm trying to find an apartment I can afford."

"Is anyone helping you?"

"My family members help as best they can."

"That's good. I'm glad you're back home in Cleveland."

"I take my medications myself," said Pat. "Although I don't always remember to. I've got to go now, Dennis."

"Wait ... Pat..."

The call ended abruptly. I had no idea where Pat was or how to get in touch with him, or when I might hear from him again.

Kari was now awake. "Who was that?" she asked.

"It was Pat Murphy, the guy I told you I ran into on the church steps last year."

"What's he doing calling you, and so early on a Sunday morning?"

"I wish I knew."

When I had brought Pat to my parents' house after finding him so bedraggled on that sleety winter night, he told me what had happened to him after we parted at Fort Gordon.

Fort Lewis, Washington, was the world into which Pat landed in the late fall of 1971. It was to be the staging ground before being shipped to Vietnam, but by the time Pat arrived, President Nixon was beginning a drawdown of troops. Pat's orders changed and he was assigned to the Military Police unit that provided base security for Fort Lewis, essentially the size of a small city.

He immediately went missing.

Three weeks later, they found him. Pat had wandered off and eventually wound up at a monastery. The monks firmly showed him the exit after just a few days.

The diagnosis, in the terminology of his base commander, was that Pat's head wasn't screwed on right. The commander sent him to a military psychiatrist and was happy when Pat was sent packing with a psychological discharge.

But once Pat's experience with the Army ended, his mental illness became fully evident. The Army had enabled him to manage, without medication, the demons that haunted him.

His phone call to Kari and me was the beginning of a pattern of such calls, mostly on Sunday mornings and sometimes with two calls on the same day, that persisted for decades.

✏

I began my career after law school at the Trust Department of Continental Bank in Chicago. I was with the bank for less than two years when I took a job with a small law firm.

In 1978, I had been with the firm for two years when the senior partner called me into his office and said he was getting up in age and wanted to slow things down. He was letting me go. Actually, he had asked me to falsify numbers on a tax return. I questioned him and I was fired.

I stood there in stunned silence. I had never been "let go" before. Bridget was 18 months old and Matt only 4 months old. We had purchased a new home two years earlier and I had left a good job with long-term security and a great pension plan to join this law firm.

It took me some time to compose myself before calling Kari. I practiced what I would say. I felt like such a failure.

"Kari, we need to talk," I said.

"Denny, what happened? I can hear it in your voice."

"I was let go. Fired. I'm so sorry."

"Oh, my love, don't worry. We'll figure something out."

I could hear the children as they played in the background. I could hear the catch in Kari's voice that meant she was holding back tears. "I'm so ashamed," I said.

"I can go back to work until you get another job," Kari offered. "God has always provided for us and will now. We'll get through this. Trust."

Five weeks later, I received an offer from a good-sized firm in what was then called the Standard Oil Building overlooking Lake Michigan. The offer was made on a Thursday and I had one day in which to decide. Meanwhile, on that same Friday I had one last interview with another firm, and I wanted to dot all the i's in my job search.

The Friday noon interview was with a firm in Joliet, about 25 miles from our home. I figured that if the second firm made an offer, I'd take it, and if it didn't, I still had time to call the first company back. First, though, one of us had to diaper Matt and the other had to calm Bridget, who could hear the worry in our voices.

I did get the second offer after all, but the job would require us to move to Joliet and join a particular country club. And what if I were to be let go again? We would be stuck in Joliet with a country-club membership we couldn't afford.

Distracted, I made a wrong turn on the way home and we didn't get back until 3:30 p.m., much later than I'd hoped. We pulled into the driveway and I jumped from the car.

"Kari, can you handle the kids? I have to call that other place right now!"

I ran into the house, fumbling in my wallet for the correct business card.

"Weiss & Quinn, how may I help you?" I heard the operator say.

"I'd like to speak to Mr. Quinn, please. This is Dennis McNicholas. He's expecting my call."

The operator put me on hold, and I had the opportunity to listen to the music that would soon be entertaining my future clients as they waited to speak with me.

"Hello, Dennis?" came a voice.

"Yes, I'm sorry, Mr. Quinn. I had hoped to call earlier, but we had the children in the car and got lost on the way home. You know how it is. Well, I would like to accept your offer to become an associate with your firm."

"Dennis, I'm sorry. When we didn't hear from you by noon we gave the position to another candidate … hello? Dennis, are you there?"

"I … didn't realize there was a time deadline today," I said, lamely.

I stood there long after the call had ended, the phone still in my hand, tears running down my face. I had totally screwed up.

It was close to midnight when we finally crawled into bed, and even later when we stopped talking over this new twist of events. Kari drifted off to sleep while I lay awake. The light from a distant streetlight streamed into the room where the curtains had failed in their mission to join together. The soft light blended into the pastel blue of the walls. The only sound was the overhead fan and the low hum of the clock. It was nearly 2:30 a.m. when I finally began to lose the fight with my exhaustion. It had been a long, traumatic day. My body stiffened and then jerked as the phone rang, jarring me back into wakefulness.

"Yes, hello. What is it?" I said with some irritation.

"This is the operator. I have a collect call from Patrick for Dennis. Will you accept the charges?"

Everything happens for a reason. Good comes from bad. After I lost the job offer I decided to start my own law practice. We would soon have three children, Bridget, Matthew and Meghan, all under the age of three, but starting my own practice turned out to be the best thing I ever did, professionally speaking. I couldn't have done it without Kari's support.

Sure, I didn't have many clients at first, but I was the favorite dad in the neighborhood. All the kids knew that Mr. McNicholas was home for spur-of-the-moment games of softball, kickball, ghost-in-the-graveyard, red rover, football, or basketball. I spent more quality time with my children and even with their friends than many parents ever get, and I feel it was just as good for me as it was for the kids. At the time, being "let go" had seemed like the worst thing in the world. Pat calling at the same time seemed like an aberration. In the end, though, it has all made sense.

CHAPTER 14

Satan by the Japanese Maple

On a Sunday in June 1979, a Sunday like most others, Pat rang at his usual early time. I took the call, as he refused to speak if anyone else happened to pick up the phone.

"Yes, operator, I'll accept the call. Hello, Pat, how are you? … You're *where*?"

"Dennis, they said I could make one call. You're my call."

"You're in *jail*? How did you wind up in jail? Uh-huh … uh-uh … wait, who started the altercation? And you say he lives in the same halfway house? Pat, you can't get into fights like that. You need a place to live."

"I hope to get out on my own recognizance tomorrow morning."

"Well, at least that's a bit of good news," I said. "Do you have your meds with you?"

"No."

"Can you do without them until tomorrow?"

"I think so, but I feel jumpy. Listen, I have to go. My time is up."

"Wait…"

There was only a dial tone.

Kari had been listening patiently. I turned to her.

"I don't know what good these calls are doing for Pat," I said. "I mean, he talks, or rambles, and he must be hearing my words, but I think his mind scrambles them. I doubt he takes any of my advice."

"I know what you mean," said Kari. "We may never know why he's calling or what will happen to him."

"I'm afraid that if I don't take each call it may be the last one he makes to me. I have no other way to contact him. It's like he's hanging from a ledge, and maybe I'm the only one he will allow himself to reach out to him. On the other hand, he wakes us both up on the only day we have to sleep in. It's disruptive for both of us, but I don't know what else to do. I can't just abandon him."

"It's probably the social worker in me," said Kari, "but I wish we could connect with him more personally. It's so frustrating doing this over the phone. Meanwhile, just know that I support and love you for what you're trying to do for him. We need to continue praying that someday we'll understand what this is all about."

That understanding would have to wait. The Sunday collect calls continued, sometimes bizarrely.

"No, Pat, I've never been to Cleveland," I found myself saying to him one time. "No, I have never met your brother. What's his name, Martin? Martin Murphy? Doesn't ring a bell. Hold on, my son Matt is up early, he's four years old now ... Matt, why don't you go watch cartoons with the girls ... Pat? What's that, the weather? Well, it's a beautiful Sunday morning. I'm standing here looking east out the bay window. The sun is warm and filling the room with light ... What's that? No, no, Pat, Satan is not standing in my front yard! I said it was the warm glow of the sun ... No, I frankly do not think we are damned. Trust me, I think I would recognize him if Satan were out there. The pitchfork alone is a dead giveaway."

Pat persisted, and I kept trying to assure him that the grounds were free of Satan while Matt wandered back into the room and began tugging on my leg. "Hold on, Pat. Matt, what's wrong? No, no, Satan is not in the front yard. No, he is not in the tree. Those are just branches."

For years afterward, Matt would envision Satan hanging out by our Japanese maple.

Kari and I still hoped to be able to understand and help Pat. In the early spring of 1982, Pat called as usual on a Sunday morning when we were fast asleep.

"Hmm?" I said, reaching for my glasses. "Yes, operator, I'll accept the charges. Pat, how are you?"

"*Dominus vobiscum.*"

It was hard to tell whether Pat was testing my memory of childhood, when the Catholic Mass was still performed in Latin, or whether he was just off his meds.

"Yes, the Lord be with you too, Pat. Where are you?"

"At the airport."

"What are you doing at the airport?"

"I just left Mass. The sermons here are usually good. I didn't like the looks of some of the people, though. And it takes me quite a while to get here because I have to ride the bus."

"Slow down, Pat. Are you taking your medications? We have this discussion every time you call. It's really important."

"I usually take them. Sometimes I forget."

"The last time you forgot you ended up in jail," I said. "How is your health generally?"

"I'm having trouble with my teeth. One hurts like the devil and I have shortness of breath if I walk up a few steps."

"Pat, you're on Medicaid. You need to go get checked. I keep telling you to take care of yourself, right? Right? Pat, are you there?"

"Sorry, I was thinking of something else. I think I have to go, Dennis."

"Pat, stay with me. How's your diet? What are you eating?"

"I sure don't eat like we used to in the Army. Remember? We had variety then and could eat all we wanted."

"And now?" I prodded.

"When I can, I love to buy a piece of red meat and cook it in a pound of butter. I'll splurge by getting a carton of chocolate milk and a box of Velveeta cheese. That's a meal I dream about."

"Great, but if you eat like that all the time you'll kill yourself," I said. "Isn't there anyone who can help you with making some healthier food choices? And what are you doing for recreation? How are you burning those Velveeta calories?"

"I like to follow the Indians. I go to games when I can."

"That's your recreation, watching other people play baseball? Aren't you able to do anything else?"

"I don't have a car, so I guess I wind up walking a lot when I can't afford the bus."

On one of my phone calls with Pat, I suggested that he come to Chicago to spend some time with my family and me. "Come on a weekend when the White Sox are playing Cleveland; I'll get us tickets. I'm a Sox fan, you know."

Pat sounded a little doubtful. "I haven't traveled much for some time," he said.

"I'll find us a good game. You can fly in on a Saturday and on Sunday we'll go see them play. Would you like that?"

"I guess so."

Several months passed, during which Cleveland only played two series in Chicago. We had to wait until August 1984 to pick a game. Pat agreed to come and visit.

I arrived an hour early at historic but alarmingly small Midway Airport to pick up Pat. There was very limited parking in front of the terminal on Cicero Avenue, so I got there early and waited for Pat's gate to be announced. His plane landed on schedule.

I hadn't seen Pat for nearly 11 years, not since that dismally cold and wet night on the church steps, but I spotted his 6-foot-2 frame right away. His shoulders were broad and he still had a bounce in his step. His hairline had receded, although he made up for it by being quite unshaven. He was wearing khakis and a short-sleeve, button-down shirt. Red meat and Velveeta had taken their toll — he was considerably larger than in our days at Fort Gordon.

"Pat, over here," I called out over the din. "Pat Murphy." He didn't wave back, but he began moving in my direction. "How are you? Great to see you," I said, extending my hand in greeting.

"Good, Dennis." His response was like many of our phone conversations where he seemed to be trapped inside his head, a prisoner of his thoughts and fears.

"Shall we get your luggage?" I asked.

"I don't have any," he said. "Just what's in my shirt pocket."

He certainly traveled light. In his shirt pocket were two pens, a small spiral notebook, and a toothbrush. "What's in the paper bag?" I asked.

"I got you a videotape of some of Archbishop Fulton Sheen's television programs. We can watch them."

On the half-hour trip home, Pat didn't initiate much conversation and his answers were short, almost abrupt. It was clear that he needed a shower, but I was so busy trying to get him to talk and stay focused that I didn't know how to broach the subject.

"Can we stop at a grocery store?" he asked.

"No problem. Do you need something in particular?"

"I like to cook my own dinner."

I didn't know what to say. Kari was in the process of cooking up a great meal for us. Nevertheless, I took him to a big-box supermarket and Pat, without looking at me, make a beeline to his favorite aisles.

"All done," he said.

"Pat, this is it? Butter, steak, chocolate milk, and Velveeta cheese? How's your heart?"

Kari was very welcoming when I introduced them. Pat reacted to her almost bashfully. "And these are the kids, Bridget, Matt and Meg."

Pat towered over them while they craned their necks upward. I couldn't tell whether Matt remembered the phone call from Pat about Satan on the lawn. Finally, he spoke. "Hello, kids," he said. "Kari, do you have a frying pan?"

"Uh, sure," she said.

"And a plate and something to turn the steak."

"Kari," I said, trying to get her attention. I folded my hands, prayer-like, and bowed to her, mouthing, "I love you."

For dinner, Kari and I and the kids had roast chicken and rice pilaf, while Pat had his steak cooked in butter, while biting off hunks of cheese from the stick of Velveeta and washing it all down with chocolate milk straight from the carton.

After the mercifully short dinner, Pat and I sat in the living room to talk. The television was on, but he found shows either distracting or offensive, so I turned it off.

Conversation with Pat was difficult. I had to initiate most of it, and Pat was frequently distracted. However, I did manage to receive an update on his health. The news was discouraging.

Pat wanted to stay up late, so I bid him goodnight and went upstairs, where I finally had a chance to thank Kari for her gracious understanding. "We won't have to do this again," I offered.

"Don't be silly," said Kari. "Remember, Scripture says, 'When you do this …' Plus, I think it's good for the children to see us ministering to your friend."

My internal alarm went off at 6 a.m., as usual, a holdover from my days with reveille in the Army. I went downstairs to check on Pat. He wasn't in the room where Kari had made up a bed for him, and it looked as if the bedding remained undisturbed. He wasn't in the living room where I'd left him. I scoured the house, looking for him, and was about to wake Kari to tell her I'd lost him when the screen door to the patio opened and in walked Pat.

"Where have you been?" I asked.

"Outside."

"I can see that. I mean, where were you last night? You didn't sleep in the bed made up for you."

"I wasn't tired."

"You haven't been to bed yet?"

"I dozed a little. I took some of your newspapers and laid them on the grass. The bugs were annoying but the stars were beautiful. I don't sleep well in new surroundings," he added.

Kari came downstairs and offered to make breakfast. "Do you want to shower?" she asked Pat, undoubtedly hoping he would take her up on that. "I put clean towels in your room."

"No, I'm good."

Kari fixed a large platter of a dozen scrambled eggs and a pound of bacon, and offered it first to our guest, who slid the entire contents of the platter onto his plate.

I prayed that this experiment with taking Pat to Comiskey Park for a shared experience would go well. We arrived an hour early, giving us plenty of time to park and find our seats. "I'm sorry our tickets aren't better. We're down the third-base line but should be able to see some of the game. Anyway, we can have a couple of beers and talk."

"I appreciate your getting the tickets," said Pat, unexpectedly appreciative. "I'm sure they're great."

The game was rather uneventful but the Sox won. It was strange being with Pat again after all these years. He was in many ways quite different and yet, peeling back the layers that disguised him, he was still Pat, my old bunkmate.

I got him back to Midway Airport the next day to catch his plane to Cleveland. We agreed to try to make this an annual event. It was a promise we kept.

CHAPTER 15

The Messenger

ON JUNE 5, 1985, when Bridget was in the first grade and going on her first field trip, I received a call in my office from Kari. Her father had just been diagnosed with colon cancer, and she could barely talk. She put me on hold for another call, and then came back on the line to say that Bridget had fallen off the monkey bars and broken her arm.

Late that night, after we had tended to the children and to Bridget, who was frightened and in pain, and after we had finally fallen asleep, the phone rang. It was a collect call from Pat.

Although I never knew when to expect Pat's calls, and never knew exactly why he called when he did, we began to sense a pattern. While many of his calls seemed random, many of them also lined up precisely with the most trying events of my family's life.

On June 26, 1987, a day I have since referred to as Black Friday, the sky turned ominously dark, with rain and flash flooding. Kari nearly drove off the road on her way home from getting the results of her thyroid scan. My real-estate closings for the day were canceled, and when I arrived home at 3 p.m. I found Kari in the kitchen, water still dripping from her raincoat, tears falling from her eyes.

She had a tumor. It could be cancerous.

"What about us? What about the children?" she cried. "Oh my God, why is this happening? What have I done wrong? Please, help me remember that God is with us. I don't feel that right now."

The phone rang, as if on cue. I reached for it, fearing that the children's school bus had run into problems in the rain.

"Hello? ... Yes, operator, I will accept the charges. Kari, it's Pat for you."

The tumor turned out to be benign, but it seemed that Pat Murphy always called when we most needed a reminder of God. His timing was infallible.

In 1993 we brought Bridget back from the Emergency Room after she ruptured her right Achilles tendon while playing basketball for Montini High School. Pat called two hours later.

❦

In 1998, Pat called our house on a Saturday afternoon in July and asked for Bridget. This was unusual because he usually asked to speak with me. After completing her conversation with him, Bridget told us that Pat cautioned her that something terrible was going to happen but that he couldn't share any more information with her. That night one of her college roommates hit and killed a man on a rural country road in Indiana. Bridget received a call the next morning from her roommate's mother. Her roommate was locked in her room and would not come out until Bridget drove there to talk with her.

❦

As he began to prepare for college, our son, Matt, expressed an interest in joining the Air Force ROTC at the University of Notre Dame where he was to begin his studies in August. We knew he was doing this to try to get a scholarship to reduce the financial burden on us. We were supportive yet concerned. I was particularly apprehensive, given my own military experience.

I discussed this with my brother Kevin while playing golf one Saturday morning.

There had been a time when Kevin and I weren't so close. I was cursed because I was the first-born son in an Irish family. Kevin was cursed because he wasn't. There were three years between us, just enough that my friends and I were bothered when my baby brother tagged along with us, but the difference in age became less of an issue as we got older.

In a house mostly without air-conditioning, we shared an idyllic child-hood room with cross-ventilation above the open back porch in summer. There was a tree outside whose branches picked up the gentle breeze and stroked the window screens with the finesse of a harpist. There, we would talk for hours in bed, and ever after Kevin was one of my best friends, the go-to person for thorny family issues. I went to him with my own struggles over whether to join the ROTC, and he in turn came to me when he was first thinking of leaving the seminary.

"I'm afraid to tell Mom and Dad because I don't want to disappoint them," he confided. "You left the seminary, all our cousins left the seminary, and now I'm the last man standing."

"I hear what you're saying, but you have to live your life," I told him. "After all, Dad left in his second year in the major seminary when he met Mom and got married. How can they express disappointment in the face of their history?"

"Aha," said Kevin. "You seem to be expecting rational thought on this topic."

Kevin offered to give me his seminary draft exemption. Such a thing wouldn't work, of course, but it was sweet of him to suggest it. We often finished our talks with ice cream and Hostess cupcakes — "for old times' sake," according to Kevin — or a trip to the McDonald's in Oak Park where he had flipped burgers one summer.

At Columbus Park Golf Course, a Cook County public course where we first learned to play golf, Kevin and I sat beneath a tree in a shady spot near the third tee while we waited our turn.

"With Matt considering ROTC, I've been giving the issue a lot of thought again, about wars and our country," I said. "Our last advertised war was Operation Desert Storm in 1991. Have you ever noticed how the government packages these conflicts to make it seem there's no alternative but to engage? That war was over in less than six weeks, so it was difficult to study in detail, but I swear that many of our leaders are like political salesmen. They package these wars for sale to an ignorant public. They face nothing, no personal risk, except perhaps being forced to say how sorry they are if things don't work out later and they're proven wrong."

"I thought the Catholic bishops denounced that war," said Kevin.

"No, the Church leadership didn't actually express opposition. It was more of a concern that the war ran a high risk of violating Catholic principles. People continued to die during this period of indecision, if I can even call it that. Our participation in conflicts never ends. Remember World War I, the war to end all wars? What a joke! Every generation has its own war. I'm just ashamed that it took the draft lottery to force me to face the morality of it all. Because of the draft, people from all parts of the country and all walks of life were either involved in it or knew someone who was. Now a professional army fights our wars. Only a small percentage of people know someone well in the military. Wars and conflicts have become much more abstract."

"What do you think the solution is?"

"I think we need to talk about conflicts and major issues that confront our country in the same way that we judge a piece of sculpture. We have to view the issue from all sides. Too often as a nation we seem to make judgments based on immediate stimuli. We lack historical perspective. We also often elevate politicians to a level where they don't belong. They might have money and clout, but they are no more intelligent, insightful, compassionate, or ethical than most of the rest of us, yet their decisions have serious consequences for so many poor souls, military or not."

"But how do you or any of us change anything?" asked Kevin. "What's your plan?"

"I think first and foremost that I struggle with how to be a person of faith and at the same time a well-informed citizen who holds the government accountable to ensure that its decisions are sound and in the best interests of our entire country."

"That's a tall order, bro."

"I know. You're right. It's usually enough to keep up with my job and my family. I just don't ever want to be caught off guard again, the way I was when I was drafted."

My faith since the draft had descended into an unfamiliar and uncomfortable place. The road signs had been removed, or had morphed into unrecognizable forms and people. We had begun to see Pat, in his strange way, as a messenger of God, always calling when we most needed comfort, providing something divine for me and my family when all along I had been telling myself that I was being there for him so as to help him. In truth, it was the other way around. This was not the straightforward faith on which I had been raised — but it made sense to me, and to Kari, in a topsy-turvy world.

"Kevin, I believe I now have a more mature and critical faith. God is God. The rest of us — clergy, holy men and women, lay people — we're all just struggling, trying to look to each other for support and to God for the grace to persevere."

Kevin was curious about my friendship with Pat. "Didn't he call 911 one time when you guys were out and he couldn't get out of the La-Z-Boy? And didn't he fall asleep with a lit cigarette and nearly set the carpet on fire?"

"Well, you know, Pat is Pat. He's often obnoxious, selfish, and ill mannered. In all of the years that I have known him, with the exception of that night when he met Mom and Dad, I've never seen him bathe no matter how many times he visits us. I can't tell you the number of candles we've burned to try to offset that. One morning he tried to warm up coffee in a glass decanter over an open flame."

"I'm not sure I'd have him in my house, no offense."

"Well, not all messengers are heroes, and not all of their messages are good news," I said. "I think God is a master of disguise."

"Pat's sure wearing a good disguise."

"Look, lots of people see him as a weird guy with a hygiene problem who overshares his opinions in a loud voice. Okay, I get it. But I would say that my family has learned to delay an initial judgment of other people. We've come to believe that Pat is a messenger in disguise from God and that his delivery, though often garbled, serves as a reminder that God is with us and will never leave us, no matter how difficult our lives may be."

❦

As the children grew, the opportunities for us to be together as a family became fewer. It was Bridget's last summer at home, as she would be graduating from college in May of the next year.

"Maybe we can all sit and talk," I suggested while everyone was watching TV.

"Seriously, Dad, a family meeting?" said Matt, rolling his eyes. "We're not kids anymore."

"We don't have that much time left as a family under the same roof," I pointed out. "Matt and Meg, you will be gone for successive years studying in Rome. You're all in universities and have summer jobs."

"Right," said Kari. "Let's slow down and make this time memorable for good reasons."

"We can talk about what we're grateful for," Meg offered.

"I think we should be thinking about those who have so much less than we do," Matt said.

Bridget agreed. "Yes, think about how life is for Pat," Bridget said. "He's had less than we have for most of his life."

"Why can't we call *him* for a change, Dad?" Meg asked.

"He doesn't have a phone," said Kari. "And in fact, we haven't heard from him in over four months. We have no way to contact him. Maybe we can just say a prayer for him and hope he's okay. Bridget, why don't you start."

"God, please protect our friend," said Bridget. "Now let's close our eyes and each say a silent prayer for Pat in our own words."

After several minutes of silence, Matt added, "Amen."

That night at 2 a.m., as if hearing our prayers, Pat called collect from Cleveland.

୧৮

On a Saturday afternoon in July 2002, Pat was due to arrive at 12:30 p.m. on Southwest Airline Flight 74. I checked the board and confirmed that his plane had landed. I waited until I felt certain that all the passengers from that flight had exited the terminal.

Almost thirty minutes passed. I stood in line for an available Southwest agent to help me.

"What is your friend's name?" she inquired.

"Patrick Murphy."

"Hmm … well, I see that he did buy a ticket, but he never boarded the flight. Perhaps he missed it and managed to get a seat on the next? That one will arrive in two hours."

I hadn't brought a book, not having expected to spend so much time at the airport, so I dozed in a chair for most of those two hours. After that, I found a vantage point from which to survey the passengers as they disembarked from the next flight from Cleveland. Another forty-five minutes and still no Pat.

Patrick Murphy never made the trip to Chicago in 2002, or any other year. After not hearing from him for several days, his brother went to Pat's apartment and found him lying face down on the kitchen floor. The coroner determined that he'd died of a massive heart attack.

Pat was 62 years of age. His new shirt lay on the bed next to his plane ticket for Midway Airport, Chicago.

IN LOVING MEMORY

PATRICK J. MURPHY
BORN
NOVEMBER 18, 1940
ENTERED INTO ETERNAL LIFE
JULY 3, 2002
FINAL RESTING PLACE
ALL SOULS CEMETERY
SEC. 32 LOT 1646 GR.1

*May the road rise to meet you,
May the wind be always
at your back,
May the sun shine warm
upon your face,
The rains fall soft
upon your fields.
And until we meet again,
may God hold you
in the hollow of His hand.*

ARRANGEMENTS BY
SCHULTE & MAHON-MURPHY
FUNERAL HOME

CHAPTER 16

❧

Jack

FOR SO MANY years we relied on Pat to contact us in challenging times. When you think about it, it was strange and beautiful that a guy who couldn't take care of himself could still call at just the right moment and somehow remind us that God is with us.

But Pat wasn't calling now. We had to adapt to that reality. We would always be grateful to him for opening our eyes to the positive signs and messages that have been and are around us our entire lives.

It's not always easy. In 2009, our first grandchild, Jack, was born. Bridget, Jack's mother and our first-born child, was the first to suspect that something was wrong. Was Jack's color just a little off? Was his color more yellow? Initially we attributed her concerns to those of any new mother, but she persisted and convinced her husband, Tim. After the seemingly endless tests Jack was diagnosed with a rare disorder that turned his liver into an inflamed mass of tissue that no longer functioned. He needed a transplant.

You would think that a baby's needs, only a tiny part of an adult donor's liver, would come first, but Jack's parents were taking such good care of him that donor organs went to others before him. In all my years, including worrying about being sent to Vietnam to kill or be killed, I had never been as frightened as I was for this baby, or felt as helpless.

There were serious risks, even if a donor were found. Kari and I were considered too old to donate. Bridget was pregnant with their second child, Gracie. Tim was a match, and therefore a potential liver donor, but he would not be eligible to donate a second time if Jack rejected the transplant. There was a strong risk for Tim, too, including possible death. And would Jack even survive the surgery, frail and tiny as he was?

Months passed and Jack continued to lose strength. His liver was swollen and he was taking seven to eight different medications every day. When I took him in the stroller to the Lincoln Park Zoo or the local park, he could only watch the other children running, playing and laughing, unable to join in.

One night when he was back in the hospital for more tests, I held him in my arms, unwilling to let him go. His small body was shutting down, bit by bit.

He finally fell asleep on my shoulder. I could hear his every shallow breath. Would my grandson die in my arms?

I began my bargaining with God. Why Jack? What has he done? He's just a baby. The doctors couldn't use my liver so take me instead. Please don't do this to Jack. We've been your faithful servants. How are we to interpret this?

Bridget and Tim had fallen into wretched sleep on plastic molded hospital chairs. I moved slowly and quietly over to where Kari was sitting, quietly weeping. "God, where are you? Where is Pat Murphy now?" she whispered. "I want a call from Pat!"

"Kari, I know, I know. I wish Pat would call us and give us a sign that God knows what's going on and cares. Oh, how I long for a clear message, no decoding, just straight talk. Will Jack live? You know, simple questions like that with no convoluted answers."

I felt as if my faith had become a swift river flowing through a deep gorge, each bend presenting a new and unanticipated challenge. I was willing to grab onto anything to avoid being swept over the next waterfall, but what to grab? Would there be something to catch hold of when I needed it? When I was a kid, the rules were crystal clear, and there were leaders in abundance who would address the most complex personal and moral issues. The churches were filled with people whose beliefs were predominantly the same. I wanted things to be simple again. How did we get here?

"Look, Kari," I said. "I know Pat often called us for no particular purpose, almost like a test. Maybe it was that we needed to continue accepting his calls until we understood that the messenger and the news he carries are not always easily discerned. Maybe we are still getting messages, and we just aren't seeing or understanding them."

"But what if the answer to our prayers is an answer we cannot accept?" wondered Kari. "Will our faith be strong enough, I can't bear the dark side of what might happen, and I can't even think about a future without faith or even with just less of it."

"Kari please, your faith has always been as strong as or stronger than mine. If we lose faith, Pat or no Pat, all that's left is a dark abyss, some hopeless place. I don't want us and our family to be hopeless pawns in some cosmic chess game."

I collapsed into a chair and eventually fell asleep with Jack still sleeping on my shoulder.

⚘

Jack was being tube fed and growing weaker by the day. Tim had been preparing all this time in case he was called upon to be the donor if no other option came through; he worked out and reduced his body-mass index to the required specifications, as living donors had to be in superb physical condition to withstand the rigors of the surgery and aftermath.

The pressure on all of us was intense. One afternoon Kari called while I was in my office. I could hear the heaviness in her voice, and inadvertently snapped my pencil in half. By then we had been married 35 years, and I knew how hard she was trying to mask her tears.

"Remember when we used to go out for coffee and pie every Friday night, even when we had three kids at home under the age of six?" I asked her. "How about you and I have a date night? Just the two of us, coffee and pie."

As soon as we were across from each other at a table in the restaurant, Kari reached out to me. We sat in silence for the longest time, just holding hands.

On a Monday in May of 2011, Tim donated 20 percent of his liver to his son, Jack, who was then 19 months old. Our entire family gathered in the waiting room of Children's Memorial and instinctively formed a tight circle of chairs as if to defend us from the world, the wait, and perhaps the truth.

Jack's surgery was estimated to last between 10 and 12 hours, but it was a mere six hours later that a doctor came to tell us that the surgery had been successfully completed.

We threw our arms around each other in joy, although we knew the danger wasn't over. Jack's body could still reject the new liver. So many things could go wrong.

We took turns standing over Jack in the Pediatric Intensive Care Unit. We dressed in gowns, masks and gloves because of his compromised immune system. His small body had so many tubes running in and out, as well as down his throat. It prevented him from making any sound whatsoever as he writhed in silent pain, tears streaming down his cheeks. I folded a tissue and wiped away his tears.

In the months leading up to the transplant, Jack had to endure countless blood draws, as well as having food and medications administered through a tube. Each time he finished another procedure, his parents would exclaim, "You did it, buddy!"

On the second day after surgery, the staff received approval to remove his breathing tube. Tim was still convalescing from his part in the procedure, but the rest of us stood watching as the nurses carefully withdrew the tube from Jack's small throat. Jack opened his eyes and looked at us anxiously as we hovered around his bed. He croaked out in his toddler's voice: "I did it!"

"Yes, yes you did it, Jack."

I squeezed his hand. "Jack, is there a message for us in all of this?" I asked. "Are you a messenger, too?"

Kari had reached over and put her hand on mine. We looked at each other, and I knew she felt the same way.

I wasn't alone.

We entered on that hidden road to find
our way once more into the world of light.
My leader walked ahead and I behind,
without a pause to rest, till we were in sight
of a hole that showed some few particulars
of those heavenly things that beautify the night.
From there we came outside and saw the stars.[8]

Epilogue

AN ANCIENT SYMBOL known as the Vescia Piscis has the appearance of two circles overlapping each other. The symbol created where this overlap occurs is often called "the eye of God" or the "Jesus fish."

Some journeys have signs and mileposts that help us to know where we are, where we have been, and where we are going. Other journeys bring us to dark and uncertain places with no clear way ahead, no known destination or sense of time.

Pat can no longer call, but his effects are still felt. In 2013, Meghan, our youngest, included an essay about Pat in her job application to the Veterans Administration Hospital in Maywood, Illinois. Although she is not herself a veteran, and they usually only consider veterans for jobs there, she was called in for an interview.

"Your credentials are excellent," the chair of the hiring committee told her. "You have an MSW from Loyola. You're licensed as a school social worker. You have two years of volunteer service, and work experience in Milwaukee and here in the Chicago area. However, to be frank, you're here because of the story. Several members of the committee cried when they read about Pat and your family."

"He became like a family member, even with his idiosyncrasies and his different ways," said Meg. "Even now, years after his death, his life continues to touch us and affect us in ways we could not have imagined."

"Meghan, welcome to the VA. When can you start?"

It is now 2017 and Kari and I are continually astonished at our three children and five grandchildren. Life goes on and we are almost unable to catch our breath, as we never stop looking for signs, messages — anything available to help us hold our faith close.

Our parents, God bless them, are gone now. Our children and their spouses have experienced many of the vicissitudes of life and health. The men in my family have historically suffered early heart attacks, and my youngest brother, Kieran, was not spared. He had a serious heart attack and quadruple bypass surgery at age 54. My beloved brother Kevin, a lifelong best friend, lived healthfully enough to avoid heart trouble, only to find that he had inherited a previously undiagnosed liver defect for which there was no cure. We lost him in the fall of 2016.

Our first grandchild, Jack, will be eight soon, six years after his liver transplant.

There's an old church hymn that goes: "Faith of our fathers, holy faith, we shall be true to Thee till death." For some people, perhaps fewer these days, the attainment of that goal is more dream than reality. It depends largely on how and what our parents taught us. The quality of the home schooling by our parents and guardians plays an enormous role in laying the groundwork for us in our life's faith journey. However, as my family and I have come to learn, God's plan can take us off-road to unexplored territory where we encounter people in places that seem foreign to us. All this will challenge our faith and darken the way forward. I could never have dreamt where my faith's journey has led me. Only by making the journey and being open to the messengers sent to me have I learned the principles of life that I pray will sustain me.

The answers I ultimately found were not in a book, a sermon, or even entirely in the Bible — but rather in real people, often in disguise and speaking garbled messages. I believe that Pat Murphy, as he made his collect calls from Cleveland, was just such a messenger.

Life is an ongoing story. Joy and sorrow, gain and loss, pushing and pulling, a tug of war. Pat is gone; no calls or visits. I find myself asking, "Pat, is that you?" There is no answer, not that I expected one. That would be too easy. New messages are encrypted, delivered by messengers adorned in myriad disguises. I find comfort knowing that there are others whose lives have been touched in ways similar to ours.

Yes, Pat is dead. But, in a beautifully executed move, Pat handed at least part of his mission in our lives to his sister, Sheila. Within days after Pat's burial, Shelia left a touching message on our answering machine, thanking us for all that we had been for Pat, and she has continued a pattern of calls over the years checking to see how my family is doing and bringing us up to date on her and Pat's extended family.

My request to you, the reader, is simple. Tell me the story of the "Pat" in your life. I promise that your story will be made known, in the hopes that others will become more vigilant and able to recognize the Pat in their lives, too. Email me at GodCalledCollectFromCleveland@gmail.com for more details on a story that you would like to submit.

YOUNG PATRICK MURPHY

Dennis, the author, is the center
person in the upper row

Acknowledgments

I WANT TO express my deep appreciation to Karin, my wife of 43 years, for her support and patience over the past 11 years as I have worked on this book. The many hours I spent writing were often hours we did not have with each other or our family.

In the *Inferno* the Roman poet Virgil was the trusted guide of Dante on his journey. Our son, Matt, has been a guide and writing coach. He has provided loving but honest feedback that gave me a perspective which I often lacked while working alone as I so often did. He spent untold hours taping our conversations and his interviews of me, making notes and encouraging me to finish my work.

The respect, love and encouragement of our daughters, Bridget and Meghan, had me persevere even when I was tempted to quit.

In 2006, I finally started to put pen to paper. It was then that I took two online memoir writing courses led by Jami Bernard of Barncat Publishing in West New York, New Jersey. She took my final draft and skillfully edited the work. Her expert guidance and assistance were invaluable.

My thanks go out to John Jiambalvo, an author in his own right and character depicted in this book, for his advice and guidance over the years as he reviewed many drafts of my work and gave me feedback as perhaps only a friend of 43 years can.

I want to express my appreciation to W. W. Norton and Company, Inc., with offices in New York and London, for granting me permission to use the quotes contained in my book from Michael Palma's translation of Dante's *INFERNO*.

I would like to express appreciation to members of my staff who have spent countless hours assisting me in this endeavor.

Finally, I want to express my gratitude to the doctors and care providers who saved the life of my grandson, Jack, and others who have continued to provide care to the members of my family over the years including my daughter-in-law, Elizabeth.

Footnotes

[2]Alighieri, *INFERNO: A NEW VERSE TRANSLATION*, 27
[3]Alighieri, *INFERNO: A NEW VERSE TRANSLATION*, 27-29
[4]Alighieri, *INFERNO: A NEW VERSE TRANSLATION*, 81
[5]Alighieri, *INFERNO: A NEW VERSE TRANSLATION*, 367
[6]Alighieri, *INFERNO: A NEW VERSE TRANSLATION*, 377
[7]Alighieri, *INFERNO: A NEW VERSE TRANSLATION*, 127
[8]Alighieri, *INFERNO: A NEW VERSE TRANSLATION*, 391

Appendix

THE FOLLOWING PAGES are reproductions of actual correspondence relating to events as depicted in this book.

SELECTIVE SERVICE SYSTEM
SPECIAL FORM FOR CONSCIENTIOUS OBJECTOR

Form approved.
Budget Bureau No. 55-R0115

| DATE QUESTIONNAIRE RECEIVED |
| AT LOCAL BOARD |

Date of Mailing ____

Complete and return within 30 days.

1. Name of Registrant (First)   (Middle)   (Last)   2. Selective Service No.

3. Mailing address (Number and street, city, county and State, and ZIP Code)

(The above items, except the date received back at local board, are to be filled in by the local board before the questionnaire is mailed.)

INSTRUCTIONS

A registrant who claims to be a conscientious objector shall offer information in substantiation of his claim on this special form which, when filed, shall become a part of his Classification Questionnaire (SSS Form 100).

Section 6(j) of the Military Selective Service Act of 1967 provides: "Nothing contained in this title shall be construed to require any person to be subject to combatant training and service in the Armed Forces of the United States who, by reason of religious training and belief, is conscientiously opposed to participation in war in any form. As used in this subsection, the term 'religious training and belief' does not include essentially political, sociological, or philosophical views, or a merely personal moral code. Any person claiming exemption from combatant training and service because of such conscientious objections whose claim is sustained by the local board shall, if he is inducted into the Armed Forces under this title, be assigned to noncombatant service as defined by the President, or shall, if he is found to be conscientiously opposed to participation in such noncombatant service, in lieu of such induction, be ordered by his local board, subject to such regulations as the President may prescribe, to perform for a period equal to the period prescribed in section 4(b) such civilian work contributing to the maintenance of the national health, safety, or interest as the local board pursuant to Presidential regulations may deem appropriate and any such person who knowingly fails or neglects to obey any such order from his local board shall be deemed, for the purposes of section 12 of this title, to have knowingly failed or neglected to perform a duty required of him under this title."

SSS Form 150 (Revised 8-31-68). (Previous Editions Obsolete)

(1)

Midwest Committee

M C
D C

for Draft Counseling

711 South Dearborn Street, Chicago, Illinois 60605—312/427-3350

Regional office of CCCO / An Agency for Military and Draft Counseling

National office: 2016 Walnut Street, Philadelphia, Pennsylvania 19103—215/568-7971

West Coast office: 437 Market Street, San Francisco, California 94105—415/397-6917

LETTERS IN SUPPORT OF CO CLAIM
November 19, 1968

One way the conscientious objector can strengthen his claim to classification as a conscientious objector is to secure good letters supporting his stand and submit them to his draft board. These letters should be sent along with the Special Form for Conscientious Objector (SSS Form 150), if at all possible; but they can be submitted later. They become a part of the CO's file. Good supporting letters are invaluable.

HOW MANY LETTERS? We suggest 5 or 6 letters of good quality.

WHOM SHALL I ASK? Get letters from your teachers, employers, neighbors, ministers, and from your friends and family friends who know you well. We suggest including not more than two or three letters from relatives. Letters from nonpacifists are important. If a reference disagrees with the CO's position but believes in his sincerity he should say so in his letter; such letters are probably given more weight by draft boards.

Letters one page in length are more likely to be read than longer ones. It is considered polite to address the letter to "The Chairman, Local Draft Board" rather than "To Whom It May Concern" or to the CO himself. Supporting letters should, however, be sent to the CO, who may be sending his claim or other material to his local board at the same time. Or, he may decide the letter would not be helpful for some reason and decide not to submit it. If the letter is typed, a carbon copy for the CO's own file is very helpful. Otherwise, the CO should photocopy the supporting letters before sending them in.

CONTENTS OF A GOOD SUPPORTING LETTER

References should be aware that Selective Service is interested in three points: Is the CO sincere? Has his conduct been consistent with his claim since he became a CO? Is his claim based on religious belief, however broadly defined?

The first two points are clear. The third presents no problem if the CO participates in a religious group. If he believes in God, there is no problem even though he belongs to no religious group. Even if he is agnostic, Selective Service is obliged by court decisions to consider him religious if he holds a belief which takes the place in his life that a belief in God takes in the life of a more orthodox person. Letters should express the writer's belief--

1) in the sincerity of the CO making the claim;

2) that the general character of the CO's life and thought is consistent with his stand as a CO to war (or, if his beliefs have recently changed or matured, that this development is genuine and consistent with more basic values);

3) that his stand in opposition to participation in war is "by reason of his religious training and belief."

209 Grace Tower
Univ. of Notre Dame
Notre Dame, Ind. 46556
March 16, 1970

Dear

How's everything going? Well, I hope. I'm in my second semester of
law school here at Notre Dame and I haven't flunked out and I'm still interested so I'd have to say those are good signs. I am writing because I
need your help with a problem. After quite a bit of thinking and praying
I've come to the conclusion that I cannot allow myself to enter into the
Armed Forces in any capacity. Therefore I am applying for a Conscientious
Objector classification. I would ask that you read the enclosed sheets
and, if you will, write a letter of support for me.

This is a summary of the basis of my CO claim:
According to the mandates of my religion (what I feel them to
be) as they are manifest in the doctrines of the Roman Catholic
Church and the New Testament and according to the mandates of my
conscience I find that I am unable to participate in any of the
forms of modern warfare as we now know them. I love my country
and the principles she stands for but I must express my patriotism in some other way. Therefore I am applying for 2 years alternative government service.
Christ said,"Love your enemies; do good to those that hate you,
(Matt.V;40-41);... love one another, as I have loved you,...(b)y
this all men will know that you are my disciples...(JohnXIII;34-35).
St. John said,"(l)et us not love in word nor in tongue, but in
deed and in truth(1st Epistle of John III;17-18). I can be of no
use to myself or to my country if I allow my decisions to be influenced by what others say or think about me. Some may think me
a coward at the very least, but I am doing what I sincerely believe I must do. Every person is entitled to his own opinion
about me.

This may sound very idealistic and unrealistic but I have no control
over that. If I am forced to I believe that I will refuse to be inducted.
I can then be convicted of a felony. So the consequences of my decision
could be quite serious.

I would appreciate your help greatly. If you do decide to write this
letter please send it to my home address before March 31 if that is possible. Mail it later if necessary. My address (home) is:
819 So. Humphrey
Oak Park, Ill. 60304

Please observe the directions for the writing of this letter. Thank
you very much. Good luck and God Bless you.

IMMACULATE HEART OF MARY SEMINARY
ST. MARY'S COLLEGE · TERRACE HEIGHTS
WINONA, MINNESOTA 55987
PHONE: 8-4349

OFFICE OF THE RECTOR

March 19, 1970

The Chairman
Local Draft Board

Dear Sir:

I can appreciate the unenviable position which you hold and the onerous task of judging the validity of the claims of young men who for one reason or another seek exemption from their Selective Service obligations. Personally I have mixed feelings in regard to their claims, but I must admit that in many instances my own feelings precede facts and accurate information in each case.

A former college counselee whom I have known for about four years has asked that I write this letter to vouch for the sincerity of his claim to a CO status. I do not argue for the position he has assumed, but I can say from personal knowledge of Dennis McNicholas that if anyone is sincere in stating his beliefs, this man is.

He is a religious person and his beliefs are not superficial. What he is requesting of you is nothing more than a logical consequence of the life that he has been leading. So his request does not surprise me. He lives his convictions and he has given literal acceptance to the words of Jesus, "Love your enemies: do good to those that hate you."

Dennis McNicholas is a person of a tender conscience, but that is is not to say that he is soft-hearted. During his senior year in college he served as resident assistant to a faculty hall counselor and he operated a tight-ship. He is compassionate and still he is realistic and practical. It is because of his personal integrity and honesty that I can vouch for his sincerity in his opposition to participating in a war.

The position which he has taken is one which can be reconciled to the teachings of the Catholic Church of which he is a member. In the statement of the United States Conference of Catholic Bishops issued in 1969 on the matter of conscientious objection to war, the American bishops quoted a decree of the II Vatican Council urging "... humane provision for the care of those who for reason of conscience refuse to bear arms, provided, however, they accept some other form of service to the human community."

With every good wish, I am

Sincerely yours,

St. Catherine of Siena Rectory
Thirty-Eight North Austin Boulevard
Oak Park, Illinois

March 20, 1970

Chairman
Local Draft Board

Dear Mr. Chairman:

This letter is to support the application of Dennis McNicholas for classification as a conscientious objector.

I have known Dennis for almost five years as a priest of his parish, a counselor, and a friend. I can vouch for the sincerity of his position on this point. It is consonant with his psychological and religious profile as I have come to know it. Dennis is a highly principled young man who transfers his convictions into a very idealistic Christian and extremely sensitive approach to life. This has been my observation over the past years.

I have no doubt about the sincerity and deep feeling of his conscientious objector position. I, personally, do not share this posture toward military service with him, nor have I encouraged it. However, I find that I must respect its depth and sincerity. It is my understanding that Dennis is intent on giving two years of alternative government service.

I have therefor given this letter of support to his position and application and hope that you would similarly honor it.

Cordially,

Notre Dame Law School
Notre Dame, Indiana 46556

TELEPHONE 283-6826

March 24, 1970

Local Board No. 104
Selective Service System
7227 W. Roosevelt Road
Forest Park, Illinois 60130

Re: McNicholas, Dennis J.

Gentlemen:

Let me identify myself by saying that I am a Roman Catholic priest
and a member of the law faculty of the University of Notre Dame.
This letter is being written in support of the request of Dennis
J. McNicholas for classification as a conscientious objector.

Mr. McNicholas is presently a student at the Notre Dame Law
School, and I have recently had frequent occasions to talk with
him concerning his religious beliefs, especially as they pertain
to questions of war and military service. In order to assist
you in evaluating my remarks, it may be well for me to state
that I have served, as an enlisted man, in the United States Army
and that I am not a pacifist.

Dennis McNicholas comes from a family in which the Christian
faith is a living reality, and he has attended Catholic schools
at all stages of his education. One uncle is a priest of the
Archdiocese of Chicago, and a brother is currently studying for
the priesthood. Dennis McNicholas himself was at one time a
student in a seminary program.

But Christian faith – faith in the person of Christ and His
Message – does not come automatically to a person. There is a
process of growth from the faith of a child to the personal
commitment of the adult, and this process of growth can be
traced in the life of Dennis McNicholas. At the crucial periods
of his life, he has had to face the demands of Christ and of His
message and make his own very personal and mature response. This
he has done. It must be emphasized that Mr. McNicholas's
opposition to war in any form is not a sudden
conclusion unrelated to his past. Rather, his personal opposition,
to war is an integral part of this growth process in his
religious commitment.

-2-

Dennis McNicholas possesses a strong commitment to the Christian faith and the person of Christ. This faith is the most important fact in his life, and his actions are taken in the light of this faith. He is not a "Sunday only" Christian; he is a person whose entire life is lived in an attempt to respond personally to the Word of God spoken to him as an individual person. You and I may not agree with Mr. McNicholas, but it is not necessary that we do so. The only thing necessary, for him to be entitled to the classification as a conscientious objector, is that on the basis of his religious belief and training he is conscientiously opposed to participation in war in any form.

The sincerity of his religious conviction and commitment should be apparent to all who know Dennis McNicholas. And his decision to take a stand as one conscientiously opposed to war has not been an easy decision for him to reach. It has come only after a long period of reflection, reading, and prayer. He well understands the responsibility of the Christian to be a man of service to his community and to his fellow citizens. The tension between his opposition in conscience to war and his recognition of the responsibilities of a citizen is apparent in his answers to the questions on Form 150, and this evidences both the difficulty and the sincerity of his decision.

I have read Mr. McNicholas' answers to the questions on Form 150, and the position which he has taken with regard to war and military service clearly represents a legitimate tradition within the Catholic Church. The Second Vatican Council reaffirmed the legitimacy of this tradition for Roman Catholics when it stated that "it seems right that laws make humane provisions for the case of those who for reasons of conscience refuse to bear arms, provided, however, that they agree to serve the human community in some other way." (Pastoral Constitution on the Church in the Modern World.)

In conclusion, let me state that, as a Catholic priest, I am firmly convinced that Mr. McNicholas is sincere in his statement that he is opposed in conscience to participation in war, and I am also without hesitation in affirming that his opposition is based upon his religious training and belief.

If I can be of any further help to you, please do not hesitate to contact me.

Sincerely yours,

(Rev.) William M. Lewers, C.S.C.
Professor of Law

Dennis McNicholas
819 So. Humphrey
Oak Park, Ill. 60304

DEPARTMENT OF POLITICAL SCIENCE

SAINT MARY'S COLLEGE, Winona, Minnesota 55987

26 March 1970

Dear Mr. McNicholas:

Well Easter vacation has finally arrived and I can sit down to answer your letter requesting my support of your application for classification as a conscientious objector. I must agree that your request was not only rather unusual, but also rather surprising and unexpected. My response, though perhaps not unexpected, will not be exactly what you wanted.

After reading and re-reading your letter several times, I have decided that I cannot, in good conscience, write a letter in support of your request for CO status. There are several reasons for my decision — none of which is related to either your honesty or your personal courage — or, for that matter, or your religious convictions.

First, if your letter properly mirrors the process by which you came to your decision, then I have to question the logic of that reasoning. You avow a love of our country and its principles, but you reserve the right to express your "patriotism" as you see fit. This indicates to me either selfishness or a lack of depth in allegiance to our country, or perhaps a faulty appreciation of your responsibilities as a citizen of the United States.

Second, you indicate a distinct aversion to "any of the forms of modern warfare as we know them". This fearsome weapon argument — is pure equivocation, which you, as a law student, certainly ought to recognize. Granted, we can make a bigger bang these days, but man has making war for years with blunt instruments, sharp instruments, fire and lime, boiling oil, explosives, etc. Even chemical and biological warfare find their roots in the age-old practice of poisoning wells or springs. So I reject this 'horrendous modern weapons' theme as both illusory and self-deluding.

SAINT MARY'S COLLEGE, Winona, Minnesota 55987

DEPARTMENT OF POLITICAL SCIENCE

Third, before raising your objection to the "forms of modern warfare," you state that you could not allow yourself "to enter the Armed Forces in any capacity." This statement would appear to obviate the need for any modern weapons argument. And it indicates, I believe, a lack of understanding of the immeasurable contribution made by non-combat forces. Nowhere have I seen greater selflessness, love, and humanitarian devotion to man (which you espouse) than that displayed by the medics, chaplains, and other non-trigger pullers "with whom I served in two wars.

Finally, your contingent decision to refuse induction if not granted CO status is most disturbing. My far less than exemplary past is spotted with indiscretion and wrongdoing, but I don't recall even encouraging, either directly, or indirectly through silence, the commission of a felony. Knowing you contemplate this step, I must advise you against it. Those who blithely counsel and encourage such action by others may feel no responsibility for the ultimate decision, and consequent results. But I would! As a student of the law (and a future officer of the court) you know the basic premise of our system that when the individual has "exhausted all remedies" then he accepts the final decision. To do otherwise is to flaunt the law — an expression of disbelief in our system.

I've tried to be honest in this reply — as you'd want me to be. Think it over. This is an important decision you are making — one of lasting impact. I want you to make that decision on the basis of reasoned judgement, and not as an emotionally rationalized avoidance of an unpleasant responsibility.

Most sincerely,

HOLY
NAME
Cathedral

March 27, 1970

The Chairman, Local Draft Board

Dear Sir,

My association with Dennis McNicholas spans the past nine years. I knew him first as his teacher and then later as his counselor. Because of this close association I feel That I can, and must, attest to Dennis' sincerity. In our frequent and intimate interviews I do not recall ever having had to doubt or suspect his integrity. To say that this lad is a most genuine and conscientious person is to understate the fact.

For this reason I must accept Dennis' present decision as a very honest declaration of his conscience, even though I cannot say that I necessarily agree with his position. I emphatically declare that I do not want to go on record as being a protagonist of conscientious objection to war. Such is not the fact. But I do regard Dennis very highly as an honest and wholesome person, and I must respect his opinion. To my mind his present situation merely reflects the conscientious approach h e follows relative to any important decision affecting his principles of living. His need to be a conscientious objector would seem to be totally consistent with his philosophy of life and his spiritual values.

I knew Dennis also in the capacity of spiritual advisor. So I do appreciate the nature and depth of his religious convictions. When he says he cannot participate in any form of modern warfare because of his religious beliefs, I feel he is manifesting a very real and delicate phase of his personality. I believe he is saying what he sincerely feels he must say. In no way do I feel that Dennis McNicholas is representing himself dishonestly .

Sincerely,

730 North Wabash Avenue, Chicago, Illinois. · 60611 · SUperior 7-8040

Name: MC NICHOLAS, Dennis John

SS No.

Date: 30 September 1970

```
{
{  LOCAL BOARD NO. 104
{  SELECTIVE SERVICE SYSTEM
{  7227 WEST ROOSEVELT ROAD
{  FOREST PARK, ILL. 60130
{_____Local Board Stamp_____}
```

Mr. Dennis J. Mc Nicholas
819 South Humphrey Avenue
Oak Park, Illinois 60304

Dear Mr. Mc Nicholas:

Your request for a personal appearance before this local board is hereby acknowledged.

☐ You will be notified of a date for your personal appearance.

☒ Your appearance is scheduled for 27 October 1970
at 8:30 P.M. in the local board office.

If you have NEW EVIDENCE pertinent to your case, please put it in writing and send it to the local board prior to the above date. This will give the board time to study it and you can discuss it with them at your appearance.

Regulations permit the local board to impose limitations on the time you may have for your appearance. Therefore, you should plan your presentation beforehand, making it brief and concise. The local board may, at its discretion, permit any person to appear with you or on your behalf, but they may not permit you to be represented by an attorney or legal counsel other than the regularly appointed Government Appeal Agent acting in his official capacity.

Very truly yours,

BY ORDER OF THE LOCAL BOARD

(Mrs) Helen S. Kelly

PM-2931 (Revised 5 Dec. 1969)

110

SELECTIVE SERVICE SYSTEM

ADVICE OF RIGHT TO PERSONAL APPEARANCE AND APPEAL

> LOCAL BOARD NO. 104
> SELECTIVE SERVICE SYSTEM
> 7222 WEST ROOSEVELT ROAD
> FOREST PARK, ILL. 60130
>
> (Local Board Stamp)

Mr. Dennis J. McNicholas
819 S. Humphrey Avenue
Oak Park, Ill. 60304

> (Date of mailing)
>
> Oct. 25, 1970
>
> (Month) (Day) (Year)
>
> Selective Service No.

Enclosed is your Notice of Classification (SSS Form 110). Your right to ask for a personal appearance before your local board and your right to ask for an appeal to the State Appeal Board is prescribed on the reverse side of the Notice of Classification. Your request for either a personal appearance before your local board or an appeal to the State Appeal Board must be made in writing to his local board within _____30_____ days from the date of mailing, as shown above and as shown on the SSS Form 110.

Your local board has available a Government Appeal Agent to advise you concerning your right to a personal appearance, your right of appeal, or any other procedural right or process. The Appeal Agent or the Associate Government Appeal Agent will give you advice only on Selective Service matters or on appeals.

If you should desire a meeting with him this local board office will arrange a time and place for such meeting upon request.

(signature)

(Member, Executive Secretary or Clerk of Local Board)

SELECTIVE SERVICE SYSTEM

This is your Notice of Classification, notifying you of the determination of your selective service local board that you have been classified 1-A, in accordance with Selective Service Regulations. The various classifications are described on the reverse side of this communication. You are required to have a Notice of Classification in your personal possession.

When a subsequent Notice of Classification is received you should destroy the one previously received, retaining only the latest.

**FOR INFORMATION AND ADVICE
GO TO ANY LOCAL BOARD**

(Sign here)

SELECTIVE SERVICE SYSTEM

NOTICE OF CLASSIFICATION

Dennis   J. McNicholas

Classified in Class
1-A

and to remain therein until

(until Month, Day, Year)

☐ by Local Board
☐ by Appeal Board
vote of
☐ by President   10-26-70

(signature)

(Member or clerk of local board)

SSS Form 110 (Rev. 6-15-67)

LOCAL BOARD NO. 104
SELECTIVE SERVICE SYSTEM
7222 WEST ROOSEVELT ROAD
FOREST PARK, ILL. 60130

SELECTIVE SERVICE SYSTEM

ORDER TO REPORT FOR INDUCTION

Approval Not Required.

LOCAL BOARD NO. 104
SELECTIVE SERVICE SYSTEM
7227 WEST ROOSEVELT ROAD
FOREST PARK, ILL. 60130
(LOCAL BOARD STAMP)

The President of the United States,

To

Mr. Dennis John Mc Nicholas
316 E. Harrison
Lombard, Illinois 60148

4 December 1970

(Date of mailing)

SELECTIVE SERVICE NO.

GREETING:

You are hereby ordered for induction into the Armed Forces of the United States, and to report

at _____ 7227 WEST ROOSEVELT ROAD _____ FOREST PARK, ILLINOIS _____ 60153

(Place of reporting)

on _____ 18 December 1970 _____ at _____ 6:15 A.M. _____

(Date) (Hour)

for forwarding to an Armed Forces Induction Station.

(Member, Executive Secretary, or Clerk of Local Board)

IMPORTANT NOTICE
(Read Each Paragraph Carefully)

If you are so far from your own local board that reporting in compliance with this Order will be a serious hardship, go immediately to any local board and make written request for transfer of your delivery for induction, taking this Order with you.

IF YOU HAVE HAD PREVIOUS MILITARY SERVICE, OR ARE NOW A MEMBER OF THE NATIONAL GUARD OR A RESERVE COMPONENT OF THE ARMED FORCES, BRING EVIDENCE WITH YOU. IF YOU WEAR GLASSES, BRING THEM. IF MARRIED, BRING PROOF OF YOUR MARRIAGE. IF YOU HAVE ANY PHYSICAL OR MENTAL CONDITION WHICH, IN YOUR OPINION, MAY DISQUALIFY YOU FOR SERVICE IN THE ARMED FORCES, BRING A PHYSICIAN'S CERTIFICATE DESCRIBING THAT CONDITION, IF NOT ALREADY FURNISHED TO YOUR LOCAL BOARD.

Valid documents are required to substantiate dependency claims in order to receive basic allowance for quarters. Be sure to take the following with you when reporting to the induction station. The documents will be returned to you. (a) FOR LAWFUL WIFE OR LEGITIMATE CHILD UNDER 21 YEARS OF AGE—original, certified copy or photostat of a certified copy of marriage certificate, child's birth certificate, or a public or church record of marriage issued over the signature and seal of the custodian of the church or public records; (b) FOR LEGALLY ADOPTED CHILD—certified court order of adoption; (c) FOR CHILD OF DIVORCED SERVICE MEMBER (Child in custody of person other than claimant)—(1) Certified or photostatic copies of receipts from custodian of child evidencing serviceman's contributions for support, and (2) Divorce decree, court support order or separation order; (d) FOR DEPENDENT PARENT—affidavits establishing that dependency.

Bring your Social Security Account Number Card. If you do not have one, apply at nearest Social Security Administration Office. If you have life insurance, bring a record of the insurance company's address and your policy number. Bring enough clean clothes for 3 days. Bring enough money to last 1 month for personal purchases.

This Local Board will furnish transportation, and meals and lodging when necessary, from the place of reporting to the induction station where you will be examined. If found qualified, you will be inducted into the Armed Forces. If found not qualified, return transportation and meals and lodging when necessary, will be furnished to the place of reporting.

You may be found not qualified for induction. Keep this in mind in arranging your affairs, to prevent any undue hardship if you are not inducted. If employed, inform your employer of this possibility. Your employer can then be prepared to continue your employment if you are not inducted. To protect your right to return to your job if you are not inducted, you must report for work as soon as possible after the completion of your induction examination. You may jeopardize your reemployment rights if you do not report for work at the beginning of your next regularly scheduled working period after you have returned to your place of employment.

Willful failure to report at the place and hour of the day named in this Order subjects the violator to fine and imprisonment. Bring this Order with you when you report.

SSS Form 252 (Revised 4-28-65) [Previous printings may be used until exhausted.]

Re: McNICHOLAS, Dennis John
SSS No.
3SN(70)1173 ;

SELECTIVE SERVICE SYSTEM

LOCAL BOARD NO. 104
SELECTIVE SERVICE SYSTEM
7227 WEST ROOSEVELT ROAD
FOREST PARK, ILL. 60130
(LOCAL BOARD STAMP)

24 May 1971

Mr. Dennis J. McNicholas
316 East Harrison
Lombard, Ill. 60148

Dear Sir:

This is to inform you that your Order to Report to Report
for Induction into the Armed Services of the United States
has been amended to read:

"You are to report for Induction to the V.F.W. Hall,
424 South DesPlaines Avenue, Forest Park, Illinois
on 16 June 1971, at 6:15 A.M."

Very truly yours,

FOR LOCAL BOARD No. 104

(Mrs.) Marcella G. Walker,
(Mrs.) Marcella G. Walker,
Exec. Sec'y.

MGW
Encl. SW-5278

113

Dear Kori.
IF IT WAS
A SIMPLE
FRACTURE I
WOULD AGRAII
REMOVAL IN
SIX WEEKS.
BUT IT IS NOT
AND I WOULD
NOT REMOVAL
BEFORE BEFOR
8 OR 9 WEEKS
PAT

NORTHFIELD, OHIO
5/8/88

Dear Dennis:

I COULD NOT GET A FEW MASSES SAID FOR KEKI'S RECOVERY, THE EARLIEST AVAILABLE WAS A FEW MONTHS FROM NOW.

I TRIED TO REACH MY OUTPATIENT DOCTOR, HE IS ONLY IN ON TUESDAYS AND FRIDAYS, I WILL CALL HIM THIS WEEK.

ENCLOSED IS THE ARTICLES FROM THE JESUIT MAGAZINE.

SINCERELY YOURS

115

P O BOX 305
NORTHFIELD
OHIO
5/16/88

DEAR DONNY:
   I SAID 30 ROSARIES
FOR KERI. (4,545
HAIL MARIES)
   I WILL BE
CONTACTING MY
OUTPATIENT DR.
ON TUESDAY, TO
SEE WHETHER HE
AGREES WITH MY
TREATMENT PLAN.
IF HE DOES NOT
I WILL REQUEST
A HEARING.

(OVER)

DID YOU READ
THE ARTICLES
I SENT YOU.
I AM GOING TO
SUBSCRIBE TO
AMERICA, AND
IF YOU ENJOYED
THE ARTICLES I
WILL SEND YOU
THE MAGAZINES
AFTER I HAVE
READ THEM.

SINCERELY

Pat

1878 E, 89 s
CLEVE. O.
1/12/89

Dear Dennis:

IT IS NICE TO HEAR THAT THE CHILDREN HAVE A GOOD AMOUNT OF ACTIVITIES. MY FAVORITE IS GIRLS BASEBALL. FOR SEVEN INNINGS THE 7TH & 8TH GRADERS AVERAGE SCORES OF 18—15. THERE ARE SEVERAL ERRORS EACH INNING, AND IT SEEMS THE TEAMS WITH THE MOST SPEEDY RUNNERS WIN.

I JUST STOPPED TO SEE MY FATHER. HE IS 88 YEARS OF AGE AND HAS A HARD TIME GETTING TO MASS.

I ATTENDED MY YOUNGEST NIECE'S CONFIRMATION. THE BISHOP WAS IN ROME SO THE ABBOT FROM BENEDICTINE HIGH SCHOOL WAS DELEGATED.

I WENT TO A FEW SECURITY COMPANYS BUT THEY DID NOT LIKE MY MENTAL HISTORY.

I REMEMBER OUR DISCUSSING HOW I COULD PREVAIL AT A PROBABLE CAUSE HEARING, OVER A FEW MONTHS. THEN I MENTIONED TO BRIDGET THAT IF SHE HAD THE TIME WOULD SHE SAY A FEW PRAYERS FOR ME. AFTER THAT I WAS OUT OF THE HOSPITAL IN A FEW WEEKS. I GUESS THE PRAYERS OF THE INNOCENT ARE OF GREAT AVAIL.

I HOPE I FIND WORK SOON. THE DIOCESES JUST LAID OFF SEVERAL PERSONS AT THE DIOCESE HEADQUARTERS. THEY WERE FROM THE CATHOLIC PAPER. THERE WERE SOME PEOPLE FROM THE NEWS-PAPER UNION WHO PICKETED THE CHANCERY.

I GUESS WITH THE WAY

THE INNER CITY IS LOSING PARISHONERS THERE WON'T BE ANY HIRING OF NEW PERSONNEL.

JOHN CARROLL IS ABOUT 70% GIRLS. I WOULD LIKE MY NIECE TO GO TO A GOOD CATHOLIC COLLEGE IN THIS AREA. SHE IS IN THE 11TH GRADE. SHE WAS ON A VOLLEY-BALL TEAM IN GRADE SCHOOL AND PLAYED AT THE URSULINE NUNS COLLEGE HERE. THE CAMPUS IS ABOUT TEN TIMES LARGER THAN J.C.U'S.

I JUST GO TO CHURCH ON SATURDAY EVENING'S AND SPEND A LOT OF TIME IN LIBRARIES.

VERY TRUELY YOURS

Patrick J. Murphy

About the Author

DENNIS J. MCNICHOLAS graduated from the University of Notre Dame Law School in 1974. He lives in Illinois with his wife of forty-three years. They have three adult children and five grandchildren.

67249795R00084

Made in the USA
Lexington, KY
07 September 2017